To John Pawlik

With best wishes.

Stan Obodiac

Nov 27, 79

THE POLISH POPE
and North America

Pope John Paul II

THE POLISH POPE
and North America

by Stan Obodiac

Griffin House
Toronto 1979

Copyright © Stan Obodiac, 1979
ISBN 0-88760-098-0

Published by Griffin Press Limited,
461 King Street West, Toronto, M5V 1K7, Canada

Printed and bound in Canada

In remembrance of
Josef Rudolf Obodiak
and
Marya Godecki Obodiak Kuspira
who were born in Poland in 1884 and 1895

Other Books by Stan Obodiac

Pennfield Ridge (1949)

The Soul Speaks (1950)

No Substitute for Victory (1952)

Lord Courtauld-Thomson (1953)

This You Rejected (1953)

Cashmir of the RCAF (1955)

My Experiences at a Canadian Authors' Convention (1958)

Red Kelly (1971)

The Leafs, the First Fifty Years (1977)

Contents

Acknowledgements

Stan Obodiac wishes to thank these photographers and suppliers of photographs for the pictures in this book: Walter Uglik of Toronto; W. H. Leppek of Toronto; Mayor Jean Drapeau of Montreal; Archbishop G. Emmett Carter of Toronto; the Vatican in Rome; Janusz Uiberall of Toronto and his friend Adam Bujak of Krakow; Ed Piszek of Philadelphia; *The Hamilton Spectator*; *The Oshawa Times*; Ted Stelmaszynski of Niagara Falls; Zygmunt Jarmicki of Toronto; Janusz Kolasa of Lublin; Edward Kasprzak of Buffalo; Geoffrey Saville-Read of Regina; *Le Soleil*, Québec; La Ville de Montréal; La Ville de Québec; S. Kowalski, Ottawa; Bill Simpkins and the *Calgary Herald*; Canadian Press; *The Catholic Register*.

Thanks also to cartoonists Andy Donato and Ben Wicks for the use of their cartoons.

The author is grateful to Janusz and Grazyna Uiberall, the Zygmunt Jarmickis and Josef Kurdybelski for their assistance in checking the manuscript.

He also thanks the following people who supplied material: Paul J. Yakabuski, M.P.P.; Terry Kelly, Q.C., of Oshawa; Tony Fredo of Burlington; Jack Gatecliff of St. Catharines; Larry Sicinski of Hamilton; Leonard Jurkowski of Hamilton; Jack Nemchin of Toronto; Stan Plomish of Hamilton; John Kotowski of Toronto; Walter Mishko of Toronto; Senator Stanley Haidasz of Ottawa; Edward Piszek of Philadelphia.

With special thanks to
Mr. John Kotowski of Toronto

Foreword

There are some things that we are destined to do. They come out of our life's experience, environment, education and heritage. You prepare yourself for the tasks, sometimes unknown, which lie ahead.

As Abraham Lincoln said, "When my time comes I want to be ready."

When I wrote the book *The Leafs, the First Fifty Years* about the most famous hockey team in the world, I knew that I was the man to do it. My years in the game in many parts of the world had prepared me to fulfil myself in this task. And so it is with *The Polish Pope and North America*.

Being brought up in Western Canada and preparing myself through education, sport, war, world travel, politics and the pursuit of the arts to be the type of Canadian which no one has defined as yet, through the pages of my book about Pope John Paul II I am consciously and unconsciously expressing my long-held premise that Canadians of any extraction are as good as anybody else. Let him be cursed who thinks otherwise!

I began working on this book the very first day, October 16, 1978, that it was announced that a Pole had been chosen Pope. I had been preparing for it all my life.

When the Pope spoke to the world on the day of his enthronement in eleven languages, I understood him in seven. It was magnificent to bask in his brilliance. I had this same feeling when Prime Minister Pierre Elliott Trudeau chose Ed Schreyer to be Governor General of Canada. It means that the highest offices in the land are no longer out of the domain of the common people.

There were thrilling moments in the writing of this book. Most of the photographers whose work appears here, some of them close to the Pope, are friends of mine. My associations with His Grace Archbishop G. Emmett Carter and Senator Stanley Haidasz were great experiences. I want to thank both of them for their considerations in Canada and in Rome.

It was a thrill for me when Archbishop Carter brought back to me from Rome a coloured photo of His Holiness with his autograph. It was also most touching to my soul to receive an autographed card from Pope John Paul II with a personal message to me.

I pray that my children will grow to realize what a moment in history this is.

Stan Obodiac,
Toronto, 1979

1

The First in 455 Years

On October 16, 1978 Karol Cardinal Wojtyla of Krakow, Poland was elected as the 264th Pontiff of the Roman Catholic Church. In remembrance of his immediate predecessor he chose the name of Pope John Paul II. The world was perplexed, shaken and awed as though Halley's Comet had returned after 400 years.

Although I am a Canadian, born in Yorkton, Saskatchewan, my mother and father were born in Poland and immigrated to Canada. This tie of heritage made me feel proud that after all these centuries a Pole had been chosen Pope. In fact, I was so elated that I wrote the following letter which was published in the *Toronto Star*, the national *Catholic Register*, and a few other smaller papers.

> Clearly the hand of God is at work. With the Papacy, the Polish people have finally been rewarded. Their great Catholicity, worship of God, devotion to Mary, and democratization of man have been blessed by God.
>
> Their years of suffering are over.
>
> They paid with six million dead in World War II as the first to stand up to the Nazi horde, paid with countless other atrocities committed against them in more than a thousand years of Christianity, paid with immeasurable world-wide indignities of a hundred years of emigration.
>
> One man of Polish nativity is the winner of the Nobel Prize for Literature, another is the Prime Minister of Israel; gloriously, another is the Pope of the Universe.
>
> God does reward the afflicted.

That brief letter brought me a great deal of comment, mail and phone calls. After the election many Canadians and Americans on their return from Rome,

Four portraits showing Pope John Paul II in various moods.

where they had been for the greatest experience of their lives, told me that they had been moved by it.

On hearing that Karol Cardinal Wojtyla had been chosen as Pope we ten to fifteen million North Americans with some Polish ancestry were all caught up in a sort of spiritual levitation as though we had ascended possibly to purgatory, almost to heaven. It was a glorious feeling as though love were being shot from us by astral rays to the Man in Rome. Only a Pole born in Catholicity, who has put his palms together to pray to Mary, who has gone to Mass, and who has celebrated all the Feast Days will understand this.

Pope Leo X was only forty-six when he died in December 1521. The cardinals then chose a Dutchman, Cardinal Adrian, of Utrecht to succeed him. Like Wojtyla, Cardinal Adrian was a professor and he taught at the famous university of Louvain.

One of the main concerns of Pope Adrian was the reform of the Roman court and the ecclesiastical administration. Some of his proposed changes were so severe and revolutionary that soon there were rumours that he would be murdered.

This was also the time of Martin Luther and the rise of Protestantism. Pope Adrian sent a new papal legate to Germany to try to save it for Catholicism, but he was unsuccessful in persuading the ruling princes to ban religious innovations.

Pope Adrian was extremely disliked by the Italian prelates and just twenty months after becoming Pontiff he died on September 14, 1523, reputedly by poison.

He was the last non-Italian Pope for four and a half centuries.

Popes Since 1523

1523-34	Clement VII (Medici family)	1590-1	Gregory XIV (Sfondrati family)
1534-49	Paul III (Farnese family)		
1550-5	Julius III (del Monte family)	1591	Innocent IX (Fachinetti family)
1555	Marcellus II (Cervini family)		
1555-9	Paul IV (Carafa family)	1592-1605	Clement VIII (Aldobrandini family)
1559-65	Pius IV (Medici family)		
1566-72	Pius V (Ghislieri family)	1605	Leo XI (Medici family)
1572-85	Gregory XIII (Buoncompagni family)	1605-21	Paul V (Borghese family)
		1621-3	Gregory XV (Ludovisi family)
1585-90	Sixtus V (Peretti family)	1623-44	Urban VIII (Barberini family)
1590	Urban VII (Castagna family)	1644-55	Innocent X (Pamfili family)

1655-67	Alexander VII (Chigi family)
1667-9	Clement IX (Rospigliosi family)
1670-6	Clement X (Altiere family)

(It was during this time that the saviour of Poland, John Sobieski, was King.)

1676-89	Innocent XI (Odescalchi family)
1689-91	Alexander VIII (Ottobuoni family)
1691-1700	Innocent XII (Pignatelli family)
1700-21	Clement XI (Albani family)
1721-4	Innocent XIII (Conti family)
1724-30	Benedict XIII (Orsini family)
1730-40	Clement XII (Corsini family)
1740-58	Benedict XIV (Lambertini family)
1758-69	Clement XIII (Rezzonico family)
1769-74	Clement XIV (Ganganelli family)
1775-99	Pius VI (Braschi family)

(It was during this time that the United States became a country.)

1800-23	Pius VII (Chiaramonti family)
1823-9	Leo XII (della Genga family)
1829-30	Pius VIII (Castiglioni family)
1831-46	Gregory XVI (Cappellari family)
1846-78	Pius IX (Mastai-Ferretti family)

(It was during this time that Canada became a nation.)

1878-1903	Leo XIII (Pecci family)
1903-14	Pius X (Sarto family)
1914-22	Benedict XV (della Chiesa family)

(It was during this time that World War I occurred.)

1922-39	Pius XI (Ratti family)
1939-58	Pius XII (Pacelli family)

(It was during this time that World War II occurred.)

1958-63	John XXIII (Roncalli family)
1963-78	Paul VI (Montini family)
1978	John Paul I (Albini family)
1978	John Paul II (Wojtyla family)

2

Prophecies and Predictions about the Pope

On Christmas Day, 1978 my family and I visited Judge Lucien Beaulieu and his family in Toronto. Among his other visitors was his sister, Sister Germaine.

Wherever we went in those days following the election the conversation was about the Pope. Sister Germaine told us there was a prophecy that a Pole would become Pope just before the start of a third world war.

Perhaps this story originated in Polish folklore or arose from remembrances of the prophecies of St. Malachy, the Irish cleric who lived in the twelfth century. According to prophecies attributed to St. Malachy, there will be two Popes after a Polish Pope and then the end of the world will come. When Armageddon and the end of the world are discussed, St. Malachy is often mentioned.

The well-known seer, Jeane Dixon, prophesied that Pope John Paul II will lead the Roman Catholic Church to new heights and that he will be a great Pope. She also predicted a dangerous threat to the Pope's safety in 1980 and an illness in 1982. She felt that there might be a bridging of the gap between the Russian Orthodox Church and the Roman Catholic Church.

Why should the predictions and prophecies of greatness not be true? On Pope John Paul's birthday, May 18, in 1860 Abraham Lincoln was nominated as President of the United States. On May 18, 1910 Halley's Comet passed over the sun and people predicted the end of the world.

On October 16, the day on which Pope John Paul II was elected, in 1944 the book about Christ, *The Robe*, was published. On that same date in 1946, ten German war criminals were hanged at Nuremberg, primarily in retribution for atrocities committed against Poland and people born in Poland.

All these predictions and prophecies seem to be consistent with what a famous Polish poet, Juliusz Slowacki, wrote in 1848, over a century ago.

5

These three verses from Slowacki's poem were translated for me by Daniel Wojdylo and sociologist Jozef Kurdybelski of Toronto:

Amidst the quarrels, God strikes
An enormous bell (clarion)
For a Pope, a slavic one.
He revealed the throne.
This one under siege will not retreat
    As did the Roman.
Bravely like God he shall advance,
    For him the world is only dust.

His face is radiant with words,
    Illuminating needs.
The growing nations shall follow him
    Into the light of God . . .

The churches he shall purge,
    Their thresholds shall be cleaned.
In man's creativity, God will be revealed
    As bright as day.

3

Pope John Paul II — Who Is He?

When Karol Wojtyla was born on May 18, 1920 in Wadowice, Poland, a town of 14,000, no one could have imagined that he would become the seventh Pole to be a cardinal. But the number seven is significant; it has a mystical quality with religious overtones. To be born in May under Taurus is also portentous. This second of the zodiacal constellations propels man into spring.

In 1929 when Karol was nine his mother Emilia died. Emilia's sister, Felicja Wiadrowska, helped his father to bring up the boy. Now seventy-five years of age, she lives in Krakow and is the Pope's closest living relative in Poland.

Karol's father had been a sergeant in the army and his view of life demanded conscientiousness, diligence and subordination. Part of his discipline was to leave his son in an unheated room during the cold Polish winter. Nevertheless, he loved his son; he cooked his meals, and washed and mended his clothes.

The Church of the Presentation of the Blessed Virgin Mary in Wadowice where Karol Josef Wojtyla was baptised. His father was Karol Wojtyla and his mother was Emilia Kaczorowska. Within two blocks of this church, Karol Josef Wojtyla was born.

The University at Lublin where the present Pope often taught as a professor. Some funds from the Mazowsze and Slask concerts at Maple Leaf Gardens in Toronto were used to support Canadians who studied with Karol Wojtyla at Lublin.

One of Karol's early tutors was Professor Foryś, a German language teacher, so that German became one of his early languages. His mastery of other tongues was to follow.

At school Karol was a brilliant scholar, a good athlete, and was well liked by his fellow students. He attended Mass each morning and was head of a religious society. He also developed an interest in literature and the theatre. He was the producer and lead actor in a school troupe which toured southeastern Poland presenting Shakespearean and modern Polish plays.

Karol entered the Jagiellonian University of Krakow but his studies were interrupted by the outbreak of World War II. In 1941 his father died and a classmate, Juliusz Kydzynski, asked him to come to live in their home. During the German occupation he worked first in a stone quarry, then in a Solvay chemical plant. He helped to organize and acted in the underground theatre which served to boost Polish morale. In 1942 he began studies for the priesthood at an illegal underground seminary.

Right—Cardinal Wojtyla with the Rector and the Pro-Rector of the University.

Below—Cardinal Wojtyla listens at a University celebration and in the University Chapel.

On this and the next page are photographs of a visit paid by Cardinal Wojtyla to the Catholic University at Lublin.

Cardinal Wojtyla in a procession with other cardinals at the Catholic University at Lublin. *Below left*—He is shown with Professor Stefan Swiezawski, internationally recognized Thomist philosopher. *Right*—He shares a study desk with a professor.

During this period he maintained his interest in the arts and sports but was also active in the anti-Nazi resistance and risked his life to provide help to Jewish families during their bitter persecution.

On November 1, 1946 (All Saints' Day) Wojtyla was ordained a priest. Soon he went to Rome to continue his studies and in 1948 he obtained a doctorate in philosophy from Angelicum College. After a brief time in France and Belgium he returned to Poland.

Wojtyla seemed always to be studying and poring over books. In 1953 he received a doctorate in moral theology and in 1954 he became professor of philosophy and ethics at the Catholic University of Lublin, the only Catholic centre of higher education in any Communist country. He soon became head of the ethics department.

Wojtyla's rise in the church was rapid. In 1964 he was appointed Metropolitan Archbishop of Krakow and in 1967 he became the seventh Pole to be made a cardinal.

The Cathedral at the Wawel Castle in Krakow.

His travels as cardinal have taken him to many parts of the world. He has twice visited Canada and the United States, in 1969 and in 1976, and has made many Canadian and American friends. He has also travelled to Australia, New Zealand and Germany.

The Pope is a prolific author and has written four books and more than 500 essays and articles, as well as poetry. The titles of his books are *Love and Responsibility, Person and Act* — a treatise on phenomenology, *Sign of Contradiction* and *Joy and Hope*. The Vatican Publishing House holds the copyright on the writings and speeches of Pope John Paul II to prevent their unauthorized use.

A biography of Pope John Paul II will soon be published written by his friend, Mieczyslaw Malinski, who is chaplain at the Jagiellonian University where Wojtyla studied.

Like many other Poles, Pope John Paul II holds the Blessed Virgin Mary in extraordinary veneration, best expressed by his homage to the Madonna of Czestochowa, the Black Madonna.

In one of the most audacious moves of the church in the last 500 years, Cardinal Karol Wojtyla was elected on October 16, 1978 as the youngest Pope of this century.

Above—The Shrine of Our Lady of Czestochowa.

Right—The Altar of the Church. The famous portrait, "The Black Madonna," forms the centrepiece.

12

4

Who Elected this Pope?

The papal conclave is bound to secrecy. No one can reveal how a Pope was elected or the strategy used in the election.

One day soon after the election, I was having lunch with the German Consul General, Norbet Hebich, in Toronto and the conversation got around to the Pope. The Consul made a remark that indicated he had not had the greatest respect for Pope Paul VI, but he applauded the present choice. "The new Pope is a German choice," he added.

Why should Hebich make such a claim?

Cardinal Wojtyla had impressed German cardinals in 1974 when he said Mass at the site of the Nazi concentration camp of Dachau. Furthermore, Cardinal Stefan Wyszynski, the Primate of Poland, had been in Germany on September 20, just a month before the election of Wojtyla, for a five-day visit which included Cologne, Munich, Dachau and Mainz. This visit was of great political significance. There was a reciprocal forgetting and forgiving between the two nations in the best spirit of Christianity.

Cardinal Wojtyla, who was a protégé of Cardinal Wyszynski and who upheld the noblest concepts of Christianity by continually helping Jews to escape from their Nazi persecutors during World War II, declared his support for Wyszynski on this issue. The admiration of the German cardinals for Wojtyla is understandable when you remember that the concentration camp at Auschwitz, that outrageous defamation against Poles and Jewish Poles, lay in what was later to become his own diocese of Krakow.

With this German impetus, he was then backed by the have-not Third World countries which he has championed.

The new Pope is sure to be a critic both of Communism and of excessive capitalism. He could become a provocation to the East where freedom is denied, and to the West where the awareness of freedom's worth has atrophied.

As Erich Reprich, Toronto-based publisher of German-language newspapers, said: "Peace will have more impact now; more than just prayers."

5

The Day Wojtyla was Elected

Most North Americans remember where they were when they first heard that President John Kennedy of the United States had been assassinated. Similarly, a great many North Americans and certainly all Canadians and Americans of Polish heritage remember where they were when Karol Cardinal Wojtyla of Krakow was elected Pope.

In my own case, I was at work at Maple Leaf Gardens, which has been called by professor and alderman Bill Kilbourn the most famous religious building in Canada! My wife phoned to tell me that a new Pope had been elected. "Who is it?" I immediately asked. She said she didn't know for sure but thought it was a Hungarian.

The idea of a Hungarian Pope stunned and excited me. So the church had finally broken with the tradition of an Italian! On my way to search for a television set I tried to think of the name of a Hungarian cardinal. Mindzenty was dead. Who was there? I was joined in my search by others eager to know who had been chosen as Pope. When we turned on the set in building superintendent Don MacKenzie's office, there were scenes of Krakow. At first I didn't get the trend of the narration. I thought that since Poland was a neighbouring country to Hungary, perhaps the Hungarian cardinal had visited Krakow.

Then I was shocked and almost overwhelmed. The new Pope was the cardinal from Krakow. Afterwards we all laughed — to think that my wife, born in Scotland, couldn't tell the difference between a Hungarian and a Pole.

The experience of Janusz Uiberall of Toronto was a little different and more personal. He is a Canadian photographer who emigrated from Krakow and he is a close friend of Adam Bujak, the Pope's personal photographer, one of the best in the world. Bujak's book of great photos, *Journeys to Glory*, was a hit recently in North American publishing circles.

Janusz's wife, Grazyna, was confirmed by Bishop Wojtyla in St. Mary's Church in Krakow.

Of the new Pope the Uiberalls say, "Everyone in Krakow knew that he was a remarkable person. We knew him when he was involved with students and there is no one who could reach the young like he could."

Janusz and I anticipate that Adam Bujak will publish another book soon about the new Pope, as he surely has hundreds of excellent photographs of Wojtyla in Poland to choose from.

Richard Sacharewicz, whose father and mother own the Polish Sir Nicholas Restaurant where Cardinal Wojtyla dined when he was in Toronto, was driving a car when he heard the news of the Pope's election. "I had to pull the car off the road immediately and sit and contemplate," he said.

In a phone call I told Richard, "Get your father to find that chair where the Pope sat. It's going to be worth as much as the 'Washington slept here' stuff. You will also have to recall the menu the Pope had and reissue it on occasion."

Joe Warecki, who is employed by Air Canada, was playing golf with his brother Stan (with whom I played hockey in Seattle) in San Diego. A Monsignor Lavin told them that a Pole had been elected Pope. Joe ran off the course to the clubhouse in search of further news. For a real golfer, it needs a truly momentous event to cause an interruption of a game.

Joe often arranges charter flights to Poland and when the Pope visits there in June 1979 there will be thousands of North American Poles travelling to Poland by air.

Mrs. Gerry McNamara, who is of Polish heritage, immediately telephoned her husband to tell him how elated she was when she first heard the news. Many people are now suddenly Polish . . . but for years Mrs. McNamara's children have worn T-shirts with "I am Polish" emblazoned on them and laughed off any jokes.

It was a pleasant laugh to hear Bob Hope say of the new Pope, "Notre Dame University is now giving their football signals in Polish."

Nina is a waitress in Toronto who as a young child fled to London, England from Krakow to escape what war brought. She now speaks the accented English of Leicestershire. When she heard of the election she said, "I'm delighted by the news. I feel that finally the papacy is approachable. This rumour that the Pope had a fiancée — good. He will know how to deal with women too. My mother, who can't afford such calls, phoned me long distance from England to Toronto to rejoice with me on the election of the Pope."

One of the unusual responses to my questions on the Pope was from a young priest in my own parish of St. Timothy's in Willowdale, Ontario, Reverend Brian Pekeski.

When he first heard that the new Pope was Polish Pekeski said that there was nothing unusual in the announcement other than he was not Italian. To Pekeski that was the big news, not the fact that he was Polish. "After all," said Pekeski, who has some Polish heritage in him, "my father doesn't even speak Polish."

There must be many Canadians and Americans like Father Pekeski who are interested in the universality of the Pope rather than his specific nationality. It is true that he belongs to the whole world. From now on he must be just as meaningful to someone in Nigeria as he is to someone in Poland. Father Pekeski realized that the new Pope was a unique man and probably was the man for his time, the man who could hold détente with the USSR and at the same time uphold the democratic rights of the United States.

This viewpoint of Father Pekeski's is somewhat like my own as I am known as a "Canadian only." I was born here, I fought for my country in World War II and I passionately espouse Canadianism.

This view may also be similar to that of Peter Gzowski, one of Canada's fine writers, broadcasters and television personalities.

Gzowski's great-great grandfather came to Canada in 1832. After as much distinguished service as any Canadian he was knighted by Queen Victoria.

Like me, and perhaps Father Pekeski, Peter Gzowski grew up without coming in touch with the Polish community. After all, Peter is only one-sixteenth Polish even though he has that unmistakable name.

This lack of contact with the Polish community on the part of the Gzowskis was never more evident than when Peter's famous great-great grandfather in 1895 met the world-famous pianist, Paderewski, who was later prime minister of Poland. Paderewski spoke to Gzowski at a Massey Hall concert and Sir Casimir could not reply to him in Polish. The old man wept because he could no longer understand the language.

And yet, Peter Gzowski feels his heritage enough so that when he heard that the new Pope was a Pole he felt like celebrating.

So you see there are things which can make even the most adamant of us change.

The Honourable Senator Stanley Haidasz, MD, on October 18 announced to the Senate of Canada the news of the election. Senator Haidasz was the first federal minister and the first senator in Canadian history of Polish heritage. He gave the address which is reproduced here.

CANADA

Debates of the Senate

4th SESSION • 30th PARLIAMENT • VOLUME 126 • NUMBER 4

HIS HOLINESS POPE JOHN PAUL II

FELICITATIONS ON ELECTION

Senator Haidasz: Honourable senators, it was with great jubilation and surprise that the world received an announcement on October 16 last that the cardinals of the Roman Catholic Church, in an historic conclave, had elected, in succession to Pope John Paul I, a new pope in the person of Karol Cardinal Wojtyla, Archbishop of Krakow, Poland, where, in 1966, with many of my parliamentary colleagues in a delegation commemorating the one thousandth anniversary of Christianity in Poland, we witnessed the inspiring religious devotion, the deep, flourishing faith and religious tradition of the people. A staunch defender of religious freedom and human rights, the new Pope chose the name of John Paul II, recognizing the achievements of his two illustrious predecessors.

Canada was honoured by the two visits Pope John Paul II, as Cardinal Wojtyla, made to our country in 1969 and 1976, when many Canadians had the privilege of meeting him and being edified by his many qualities. We who had the pleasure of speaking to His Holiness were greatly inspired and fortified in the faith. Christians and members of many faiths have joined in extending best wishes to the new Pontiff of the Roman Catholic Church. I should like to associate myself with these tributes.

Honourable senators, I move, seconded by the Honourable John J. Connolly, that the Honourable the Speaker convey the felicitations and the prayers of the Senate of Canada to His Holiness, Pope John Paul II, with the fervent wish that his pontificate may be blessed in the service of men of good will everywhere.

Hon. Senators: Hear, hear.

Motion agreed to.

Wednesday, October 18, 1978

It was interesting to hear the viewpoint of the Polish Embassy in Ottawa, which would be consistent with all Polish embassies abroad.

The Polish Ambassador to Canada, Dr. Stanislaw Pawlak, wrote me that he had never met Pope John Paul II, but he expressed the opinion that the election of any new pope was an important event not only for the Catholic Church but also for the world. This seemed to be connected, in his estimation, with the important moral and political role played by the Vatican in international relations, in the field of peaceful co-operation and co-existence, détente and world disarmament.

He admitted, however, that the election of Pope John Paul II did have a special significance for Poles since John Paul is their compatriot, the first time that a Pole had been elevated to such high dignity.

The Polish Ambassador observed that because the new pope had been born and educated in Poland, he knew the hell of war and the price of peace and progress. Dr. Pawlak said that he hoped that John Paul II would continue to develop the achievements initiated by his great predecessors.

The Ambassador also enclosed a copy of a book, *The Church of Poland*, by Adam Piekarski. Some of the claims and figures in this book are not as we know them from Catholic sources.

6

The Donato Cartoon

The day after Wojtyla was chosen Pope John Paul II the *Toronto Sun* ran a brilliant cartoon by Andy Donato.

Donato has depicted Prime Minister Trudeau, President Jimmy Carter and sport promoter Harold E. Ballard with great humour and authenticity and I thought this cartoon was extremely funny. Knowing the Pope's sense of humour I felt that he too would find it amusing. So I telephoned Donato and asked him, "How much for the cartoon?"

Donato was pleased that I liked it. Then he said, "You have done a lot of favours for me; you can have it for nothing. Furthermore I might want to go to a hockey game with my son, maybe you can get me a couple of tickets."

"That's very kind of you, Andy."

A couple of days later Donato phoned me and said that Archbishop Emmett Carter, the head of Canada's largest English-speaking Roman Catholic diocese, wanted the cartoon too.

"It looks like a tough situation, Andy."

"Yeah, I know. I promised it to you and you'll get it."

I asked, "What the does Archbishop want it for?"

"He's going to Rome in December and he wants to take the cartoon as a gift to the Pope."

"Well, that's a different matter. I'll have to give it to him or I might be excommunicated."

Donato agreed to get me a couple of photographic copies of the original, which was very kind of him as he sensed that I was surrendering something that I keenly wanted.

Around the end of October I telephoned Archbishop Carter to arrange a luncheon so I could turn the cartoon over to him. In the meantime I had the original cartoon photographed in colour — Donato does not work solely in black and white as other cartoonists do.

Archbishop Carter and I met for lunch early in November at the Hot Stove Club. He was already sitting when I arrived. "Your Grace . . . by the way, weren't only kings before Henry VIII called 'Your Grace' — are you therefore taking the place of kings?"

This banter didn't upset him at all and he countered with, "Dukes are 'Your Grace' and church people before Henry VIII sat in the House of Lords, so it is not an irregular transformation."

We had a lot of good talk as His Grace had a sherry and a beer and I had a Dubonnet. It crossed my mind that he couldn't be such a bad sort of archbishop if he could drink a beer. I never beat around the bush and pretty soon we were in deep discussion about the Vatican and the church's stance.

The Archbishop was willing to bet me $1,000 that contrary to rumour from my sources in Rome Cardinal Wyszynski of Warsaw would not go to Rome as the Pope's adviser but would remain in the Polish capital. He also predicted that the church would take a hard stand on abortion. A horrible thought ran through my mind — what would have happened if Mary had aborted Christ? Archbishop Carter's personal opinion was that the church might have a lot of dialogue on divorce and that the church might have to rethink its position, as he had once told Pope Paul VI just before the government made divorce legal in Italy.

The original of this cartoon by Andy Donato was taken to Rome and presented to the Pope by Archbishop Emmett Carter of Toronto.

20

In the middle of the meal we remembered to say grace and then I handed over the Donato cartoon. I was very pleased that Archbishop Carter believed as I did that the Pope would think it was funny. He said, "Don't worry, this man is most unusual."

Archbishop Carter is a friend of the Pope's. He has visited him in Krakow and has marched with him in religious processions. He thought the Pope would come to North America in a couple of years but there are many people throughout the world who wish to see His Holiness.

It crossed my mind that since the archbishop is a good friend of the Pope's and is very prominent in the important Synod of Bishops, His Grace G. Emmett Carter might well become a cardinal, particularly since Toronto is the largest English-speaking Roman Catholic diocese in Canada.

His Grace was in Rome during December 1978 for a regular meeting of the Synod of Bishops. There are twelve members on the permanent council and he is one of the twelve.

When he returned from Rome Archbishop Carter reported that he had seen the Pope on two occasions, once for twenty minutes alone. He said the Pope got a chuckle out of Donato's cartoon. It also delighted His Holiness to hear of Canada.

The possibility of coming to Canada for another visit like those made in 1969 and 1976 seemed remote, His Grace thought. "Any visit now would have to be of international dimensions."

Although the Pope was in wonderful physical shape and was delightful company, the archbishop noticed that His Holiness was under immense pressure and he prayed that the Pontiff would not kill himself with overwork.

To my great delight, the archbishop brought back for me a colour photograph of the Pope which he had personally autographed.

"May I use it in my book?" I asked His Grace. "Is it permissible?"

"You may use it," replied the archbishop, "if anyone goes to jail it will be me."

7

The Pope as a Sporting Figure

On Thursday, November 9, 1978 I was interviewed by CBC radio broadcaster Brigid O'Toole. My spontaneous commentary ran approximately as follows.

"I wonder who the first man or woman will be to go downhill with the new Pope? By this I don't mean to suggest that the Vatican is in decay or that the new Pope has gone downhill after the unprecedented adulation of the first few days. No, I just wonder who will be the first to ski with the Pope, who as everybody knows by now is an avid skier. There is a story that last year he was out skiing with some friends near the Polish-Czechoslovakian border in the Carpathian mountains just outside of Zakopane and that His Eminence skied over the border inadvertently. He was held by the authorities for a brief time because they couldn't believe that such a young man was a cardinal or that a cardinal could possibly be skiing.

"But now, what about a Pope skiing? And who will be the first to go downhill with him?

"Will it be our own Prime Minister Pierre Elliott Trudeau who loves to get away for some skiing at least once during the winter? The next time he is in Rome, will the Prime Minister ask His Holiness if he would like to try the slopes of the Dolomites? Or, knowing the Pope's love of the Mother of God, perhaps they might ski near the village of Madonna di Campiglio? Or perhaps George Duffield, the CBC skiing expert, will take the first slide with the Pope."

At a recent luncheon with His Grace Emmett Carter, Archbishop of Toronto, we spoke about the Pope's sporting proclivities. "Do you know that His Holiness plays tennis? And do you know that there is an old tennis court at the Vatican which may be restored by the time of my visit next month? I may ask His Holiness for a game," said His Grace. It is also probable that the Polish international tennis star, Fibak, will be asked to play if he should journey to Rome with Bjorg.

Our Prime Minister can make another impression on the Pope. As a canoeist he might join him on the fast streams of the Dolomites because His Holiness loves to paddle a canoe.

As well as canoeing and kayaking the Pope enjoys mountaineering. Just prior to his election he visited the twelfth century Mentorella Monastery which is located at the top of a rugged 3,960-foot mountain forty miles from Rome. He climbed on foot to the isolated monastery which is run by five Polish friars. A few days later as Pope he was flown there in a helicopter. The Associated Press reported that the Pope said, ''This is a spot where man is naked before God. It is a spot far from everything but at the same time close to nature, where one speaks confidentially with God.''

What could be a better summation of the reason to climb?

Perhaps His Holiness's supreme gesture to sport was made when he rescheduled his inauguration to avoid a conflict with television coverage of the afternoon soccer matches. Can you imagine what this meant to soccer-mad Italians?

It wasn't the first time the new Pontiff had changed his schedule for a sporting event. In June 1978 he had a dinner in his honour as cardinal changed to an earlier time so he wouldn't miss the Poland-Brazil World Cup soccer match televised from Argentina. This game was also seen by Canadians and Americans of Polish heritage in Toronto, Hamilton, New York, Chicago and Detroit.

Right after the election I just couldn't contain myself. As Publicity Director of the Toronto Maple Leafs and Maple Leaf Gardens, I had to mention the new Pope in my very first ''Press Box Notes.''

Heading for the slopes? Pope John Paul II smiles as he accepts a new pair of skis from members of a ski school at Sulmona, Italy, at an audience.

I observed that His Holiness is an avid sportsman, being a skier, tennis player, a canoeist and kayaker, and mountain climber. I ferreted out the fact that he had skated and played hockey on frozen rivers and ponds outside Wadowice, and I rejoiced that he might be the first Pope who had been a part-time hockey player.

The Leafs' Assistant General Manager, John McLellan, said, "Why don't you send him an application form?"

I further elaborated on my story by mentioning that just south of Krakow, near the winter resort of Zakopane, there is a very fine hockey town called Nowy Targ. From this town came the nucleus of the team which beat the Russians in a recent world tournament at Katowice. I think that His Holiness would have liked to have been a member of that hockey team.

Lenin too was a skater and during his "sojourn" in Poland before World War I he also was at Poronin near Zakopane and skated on the river which ran just outside his Polish home.

If Lenin and Pope John Paul II had ever played hockey against each other, can you imagine the bodychecks and ideological banter that would have been thrown around in that game-confrontation?

Who would have converted whom?

These musings are not irreverent. This Pope is unique; this Pope is a man; this Pope is a human being.

A few days after his election, Pope John Paul II paid a visit by helicopter to the Mentorella Monastery on a mountain top forty miles from Rome.

8

The Pope and the Barry's Bay Association

Barry's Bay and Wilno are two communities east of Algonquin Park in northern Ontario where three quarters of the population are of Polish descent. So the Canadian Broadcasting Corporation sent a camera crew to interview citizens of these communities to see how they felt about the election of the Polish Pope.

I am indebted to Paul J. Yakabuski, MPP for Renfrew South, the constituency which contains Barry's Bay, for information on how the news of the new Pope affected other people in the area.

Father Stanislaus Kadziolka knew Pope John Paul II when he was a boy of ten. The priest and Wojtyla attended the same school in Wadowice. Father Kadziolka recalls that the future Pope lived with his family in a small two-room apartment above a Jewish store.

Pope John Paul II is a very compassionate man and never forgets a friend or an acquaintance. When Father Kadziolka last visited Poland in 1975 he was alarmed at the condition of his aging mother. His Holiness, then Cardinal Wojtyla, assured Father Kadziolka that he would attend the funeral of his mother if he was not able to come from Canada.

This priest has had several letters from His Holiness and has photographs of the two of them together.

Father Stanislaw Kuczaik, curate of St. Hedwig's Church in Barry's Bay, was another who had disbelief turn to surprise and joy when he heard the news of the election. Father Stan first became acquainted with Wojtyla in 1965 while in Poland on a visit. They met when Wojtyla was leading a procession to one of the numerous shrines.

In 1969 when Cardinal Wojtyla first visited Canada it was Father Stan who drove the future pontiff from Calgary to Banff in his 1967 Plymouth. It is ironical that Father Stan sold this Plymouth just three weeks before the election of the new Pope and thus lost a valuable souvenir.

After his election His Holiness Pope John Paul II still remembered the people of Barry's Bay and Wilno. Dave Brown reported in the *Ottawa Citizen* of

December 30, 1978 that Bishop J.R. Windle of Pembroke, Ontario had been in Rome and had a ten-minute chat with His Holiness. He was surprised when the Pope asked about "the boys" in the Barry's Bay and Wilno areas. He asked especially about Reverend Stan Kadziolka, the parish priest in Wilno. St. Mary's in Wilno is the oldest Polish parish in Canada. It has historic significance and has been mentioned in three books: *A Member of a Distinguished Family — The Polish Group in Canada* by Henry Radecki and Benedykt Heydenkorn, *The Poles in Canada* by Ludwik Kos-Rabcewicz-Zubkowski, and *History and Integration of Poles in Canada* by William Boleslaus Makowski which has a foreword by the Right Honourable John G. Diefenbaker.

The Pope is already becoming known for his interest in local parishes throughout the world. He asked Bishop Windle how the Kaszuby Youth Guidance Centre near Barry's Bay was faring and seemed proud that Ontarians of Polish heritage were remembering their roots.

He also asked about his old friend Father Stephan Soltyszewski of Otter Lake who had been a spiritual teacher with him at the University of Krakow, and about his Canadian "chauffeur," Reverend Stan Kuczaik.

If the Pope comes to Canada for a third visit I'm sure he will not readily pass up a visit to the Wilno and Barry's Bay region. But there are also communities in Saskatchewan, Ontario, Detroit, Chicago, Buffalo and Baltimore where other fellow Poles eagerly await him.

9

More Reminiscences about the Pope

Following the election of Pope John Paul II there were many people with nice little anecdotes to relate.

Witold Leppek, who took some of the photos which appear in this book of the visit to Toronto in 1976, says proudly, "I had a glass of wine with the Pope. He remarked on my photographs and later I sent these pictures to Poland."

Witold was placed in the enviable position of suddenly having his 1976 photographs in great demand. The Toronto *Globe and Mail* used one on the front page right after the election and on subsequent days. So did the *Toronto Star* and *Maclean's* magazine. Two newspapers in Italy ordered pictures. Then there were the people who had appeared in photographs taken with the "Cardinal" who suddenly realized that they had appeared in a photo with the Pope.

Fred Kossecki, En Route Manager with Air Canada in Toronto, jokes that he "pulled a cardinal boner" with the new Pope.

In 1976 he was in charge of the ecclesiastical party of seventeen people who, with Cardinal Wojtyla, were flying back to Europe after their stay in North America. It was in his charge to "raise" one of the seventeen from economy to first class. He chose Bishop Rubin, who is a Polish Catholic power in Rome, and passed over the cardinal who would one day be Pope.

Bishop Rubin told Fred if he were ever in Rome to please look him up if there was anything he could do for him. Your Grace, how about introducing Fred to the Pope?

Mrs. Nicholas Sacharewicz, the wife of the proprietor of the Sir Nicholas Restaurant in Toronto, which is the best Polish eating place in Canada, recalls when His Holiness ate a meal there in 1976. "He had a steak, because he wanted a Canadian meal not a Polish one. He was a most delightful man."

On October 16, Mrs. Sacharewicz was in Fort Lauderdale, Florida where that very day she and her husband completed arrangements to open another Sir

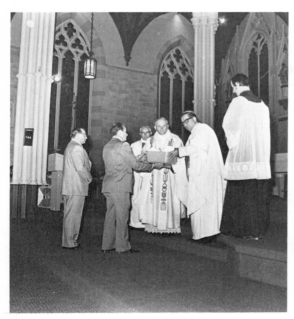

Cardinal Wojtyla celebrated Mass at St. Michael's Cathedral in Toronto, Ontario in August, 1976. In these photographs, he is shown receiving offerings, and outside the Cathedral, after Mass. Many members of Toronto's Polish community attended the celebration.

Nicholas restaurant in the United States. "There was something electric about the day; it turned out there were two Polish omens."

Reverend Michael Smith, who runs a retreat house in the Toronto area and is the chairman of the new Copernicus Lodge for senior citizens, remembers the 1969 visit of Cardinal Wojtyla as the future Pope stayed at the retreat house in Mississauga.

Father Smith said, "He had discipline, strength, integrity and was a great student. When he celebrated Mass with us his homily was on social ethics, social questions, and he asked us to build a prideful heritage in Poland. My phone has been ringing all day with questions about this man!"

It was Mr. Zygmunt Jarmicki, president of the Canadian Polish Congress, who invited Cardinal Wojtyla to Canada in 1969. Jarmicki is an aircraft designer and at present is the administrator of the Copernicus Lodge.

In 1969 he spent two weeks with Cardinal Wojtyla travelling with him to Montreal, Quebec City, Calgary, Edmonton, Winnipeg and other communities.

Jarmicki said, "There is no doubt the new Pope is a fantastic man. We were all touched by him and few could comprehend his great simplicity — he has such wisdom and such humour. At one stage of our tour we had to fly from Banff to Edmonton. The visibility was nil. The Cardinal said, 'We have nothing to worry about; we are close to heaven!'

"In Toronto we had a demonstration of his tremendous memory. A typewritten speech in English was given to him to read. Everyone thought he would read it from the script. However, even with a supposedly strange language he looked at it for a few minutes and then at speech time gave it back verbatim.

"When he was elected Pope I was jubilant. But then I recalled a 1974 article in *Time* magazine written when Pope Paul VI was slightly ill. A two-page compendium on *papabile* included Wojtyla.

"My phone has been ringing off the hook. Everyone wants to hear about my joy in the election of this man, this man we had touring Canada in 1969. You know, we can almost claim him as a Canadian Pope!"

But perhaps it was Rudolf Kogler of Toronto who was most joyous about the election. Rudolf, who is now an economist with the Ministry of the Treasury in Ontario, went to school with Karol Wojtyla for eight or nine years and acted with him in school plays. When I spoke to Mr. Kogler on the telephone he mentioned that the new Pope "had a good feeling for the theatre and was a good actor." Perhaps it is this presence which serves him so well at the Vatican and before the immense crowds.

The photograph of the Cardinal, taken by Witold Leppek of Toronto, which has been reproduced around the world.

According to Kogler, the present Pope specialized in the theatrical plays of Stanislaw Wyspianski, a Polish writer of the early twentieth century whose inspirational writings were mainly about the independence of Poland, a land often oppressed by Austria, Germany and Russia.

When I spoke to Rudolf Kogler's wife she kept saying what a wonderful house guest the Pope was in 1976 when he visited their home. "He sipped tea and ate just about everything put before him — just like a good Pole does."

World War II separated Kogler and Wojtyla. Kogler joined the Polish army in exile in Britain and eventually came to Canada. Wojtyla joined the underground army in Poland, where he helped the victims of Nazi persecution, and began his studies for the priesthood.

Rudolf Kogler went to Rome with the Canadian delegation for the installation of the new Pope and in a general audience the Pope spied him out and managed a hello. Things had indeed changed since the days when they were schoolboys and even since 1976 when the Cardinal was in his home talking over old times.

Over the years Kogler has had much correspondence with the Pope and near the end of 1978, even though His Holiness was busy with the affairs of 700 million people, he found time to write a personal letter to Kogler.

10

The Canadians Who Went to Rome

In a roundabout way Ted Glista of Mississauga, Ontario is possibly more responsible than anyone else for my writing this book.

Until I came to Toronto from Saskatchewan I had no contact at all with the "Polish" community in Canada, nor did I seek or desire it. In fact, I used to run from anything Polish; I was passionately Canadian. I never could and still can't accept the idea of anyone being English Canadian, French Canadian, German Canadian, Polish Canadian, Ukrainian Canadian, Italian Canadian or any other type of Canadian. The flash "Canada" on my RCAF officer's uniform in World War II was all that I worried about or accepted. Group Captain Father McCarthy of Dartmouth, Nova Scotia, who was head of the RCAF chaplains overseas, and I campaigned from the time the war ended for Canadians to be Canadians only. We kept petitioning Lester Pearson to introduce the new Canadian flag — a flag for all Canadians.

When I came to Maple Leaf Gardens in Toronto part of my job was to promote and publicize cultural events from the USSR, from Poland, from Britain, from the United States, from Israel and other countries, so I became acquainted with the various ambassadors, consuls-general, high commissioners, and other members of these communities.

In the 1960s and 1970s, Mazowsze and Slask, the famous dance companies from Poland, came to the Gardens on several occasions. I had to find a Polish contact who would help me to promote these shows in Toronto. I stumbled upon Ted Glista who was president of the Polish Alliance of Canada and a leader in the Ontario Polish community. He wanted to raise money for several organizations such as the Reymount Foundation and the Adam Mieckiewicz Fund and I wanted to help the Gardens. So we arrived at a happy relationship. Sol Hurok in New York and Nicolas Koudriavtzeff in Montreal, the great American and Canadian impresarios, were very pleased that I was able to sell out first nights of these shows to Polish Canadian communities. It provided leadership that enabled them to launch similar projects in other North American cities.

The tradition of centuries is inherited and performed immediately on becoming Pope.

The Pope at an audience in Rome. Cardinal Wyszynski is at the Pope's right.

It is a happy coincidence that the money we raised through the Mazowsze and Slask dance companies at Maple Leaf Gardens for the Adam Mieckiewicz Fund was used to help Canadian students attend Lublin University where Cardinal Wojtyla taught!

I pride myself on being a well-rounded man and I soon saw that these dance companies were as good as any in the world. On this basis, more than on their being Polish, I began to champion them. I started to get to know everybody in the Polish embassy in Ottawa, the Polish consulate in Toronto and Polish leaders throughout Ontario. Some of these contacts have developed into very pleasant friendships.

In 1976, just after Karol Cardinal Wojtyla had visited Toronto, Ted Glista proposed my name to LOT Airlines so that I could join a party of VIPs and press people participating in the inaugural flight of LOT to Poland.

We went to Poland in October 1976 and I had a memorable experience. I broadcast my impressions over CBC Radio and wrote several articles which were published in the *Toronto Star*, the *Globe and Mail*, the *Catholic Register*, some weekly papers and elsewhere. One such publication was the intellectual journal *Krzyk — Outcry*, published by Janusz Uiberall, a photographer I had met in Poland whose friend, Adam Bujak, was the personal photographer to Cardinal Wojtyla.

There were many further happy coincidences and I suppose they were all made possible through my getting Ted Glista and the Polish Alliance interested in sponsoring Polish cultural events at Maple Leaf Gardens. Glista modestly says, "It was you who got us mutually involved in a lot of things that benefited both of us." It also benefited some institutions in Poland. A part of the earnings from the first Mazowsze concert were given by the Polish Alliance to help reconstruct the royal castle in Warsaw and to support the Catholic University in Lublin (KUL). This contact by Glista with KUL established summer courses for students from abroad to study Polish history and culture in a Catholic surrounding. KUL was also Cardinal Wojtyla's favourite university; he lectured

The Pope lifts the Monstrance.

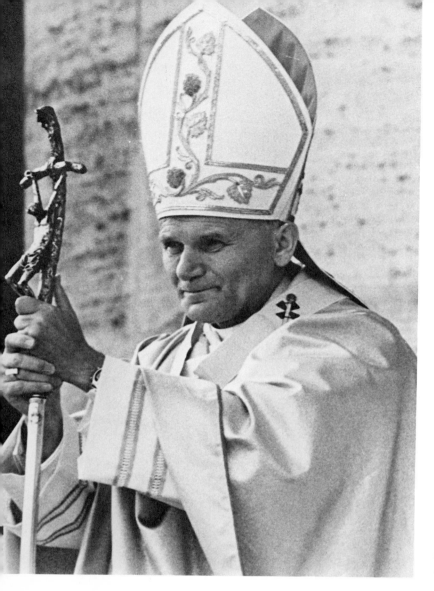

The Pope in Rome with his new Cross.

there as often as he could. So I was very interested to hear what Ted had to say when he arrived from Rome after the installation of the new Pope.

With a Polish cardinal chosen as Pope, Ted had gone to Rome as a Moslem goes to Mecca. "It was the super-high of my lifetime," he said. "There were maybe fifty of us from Toronto, fifty from Hamilton and thirty from other Ontario regions. But there were 5,000 from Poland who descended on Rome. I was amazed that the Polish Communist government was able to process passports in three hours for all those people. Even the President of Poland was there. The most incredible sight was that of the Pope and Cardinal Wyszynski embracing at the audience given for people from Poland and of Polish descent. Everyone wept openly when the Cardinal said, 'You are the Bishop of Rome,

The most famous embrace of 1978. Pope John Paul II embraces Cardinal Wyszynski, the Primate of Poland and mentor of the new Pope, during the celebrations in Rome.

but to us you will always be the Bishop of Poland and as such I pay homage to you by kissing your feet.' This was Wojtyla's farewell to Poland. He would never return to Poland except for a visit. It was the meeting of teacher and pupil, and now the pupil was Pope. It was a moment of both agony and joy. There is nothing in my life which will ever take the place of this visit to Rome.''

But there were annoyances for Ted Glista too.

Because he had served for five years as the Ontario Chairman of the Canadian Consultative Council on Multiculturalism, he recommended to Norman Cafik, the Minister of State for Multiculturalism, a list of people to go to Rome for the enthronement of Pope John Paul II. On this list was a cross-section of Polish leaders and clergy from across Canada. Similar lists were submitted by the Department of the Secretary of State.

The government ignored most of the names proposed by Glista. The Honourable Norman Cafik stated emphatically that only eleven people representing Canada would attend, since there was limited travel space available. Imagine Glista's surprise when this group of eleven arrived in Rome

Father Joseph Capiga, from Hamilton, Ontario, at an audience in Rome. ''Hello, Joe Hamilton,'' says the Pope.

with an entourage of about twenty additional people accompanying them, people who were in no way representative of anyone. Furthermore, the plane was two-thirds empty. There was no one from the Polish Catholic clergy.

Shocked at this obvious affront to the Canadian Polish community, Glista resigned as Ontario Chairman of the Council. He sent letters explaining his resignation to Multiculturalism Minister Norman Cafik and to Senator Peter Bosa.

So who was in the official delegation from Canada?

The group was led by Deputy Prime Minister Allan MacEachen. The members were: Regional Expansion Minister Marcel Lessard; NDP leader Ed Broadbent; Senator Stanley Haidasz; Conservative James McGrath; Charles Caccia, MP; Wladislaw Gertler, president of the Canadian Polish Congress; and three provincial cabinet ministers, Jacques Parizeau of Quebec, Leo Bernier of Ontario, and Kenneth MacMaster of Manitoba.

Only the leader of each country's delegation was received by the Pope. When Allan MacEachen told John Paul II, "Your Holiness, a number of Canadians have arrived to see you," the Pope answered, "Yes, I know, and among them is my friend, Senator Haidasz." This was a great honour for Stanley Haidasz to be so singled out and remembered.

Other Canadians were warmly greeted as well. Besides Kogler being recognized, as I mentioned previously, the Pope cordially received the three Canadian cardinals — George Cardinal Flahiff of Winnipeg, Paul-Emile Cardinal Leger of Montreal, and Maurice Cardinal Roy of Quebec City who is also the Primate of the Roman Catholic Church in Canada.

Cardinal Roy told the Canadian Press: "Pope John Paul II belongs to a magnificent people, who have suffered a great deal. He is an intellectual who knows modern thought and Marxism. He's a courageous man, prudent, patient, who knows how to listen." This was a generous statement from Cardinal Roy who had himself been considered *papabile*.

A friend of mine, real estate developer John Kotowski, said when he returned from Rome that it was "the most moving ceremony of my life." He brought me some postcards from Rome showing the new Pope. During the concelebration a great new industry centering on the Pope quickly began. Trade was brisk in religious medals bearing the Pope's likeness. One hawker sold medals for $12.00 — twenty yards away they were being sold for $7.00.

Souvenir di ROMA

Joannes Paulus pp II

S. S. Joannes Paulus II

A sample of the postcards that appeared almost overnight in Rome after the Pope's election.

Walter Uglik has some magnificent photographs of the Pope taken when he was in Toronto in 1969. Some of them appear in this book. Walter was in Rome with the Canadians to photograph the Pope at the concelebration.

"I had to take my photographs mostly with a long range lens. No closeups were permitted. After all, there were over a thousand photographers in Rome. But once I was in an audience of about eighty people, the Canadian delegation. I won't show a photo of the Pope if it doesn't flatter him. Some photographers seem to have no ethics; they will try to catch the Pope in an embarrassing moment."

Uglik said of his experience, "It is impossible to describe. We are lucky if we witness one such an occasion in a lifetime. There was such excitement that I felt close to God. The French were crying; the Polish were crying; the Italians were crying. Italians seemed just as enthusiastic as the Poles. They have been away from the church and some of the blame has been put on previous pontiffs, but now they feel they have a man who can be approached, who is not distant from them. '

"He is now Pope to the world. He has to say good-bye to the Polish people."

Uglik has photographs of the Pope taken in 1969 with some well-known Toronto people. Some had forgotten the Cardinal Wojtyla of 1969, so when they were told that they were in photographs with the Pope they were indeed delighted. Among these Torontonians are former mayors Bill Dennison and Fred Beavis, Alderman Margaret Campbell, Senator Stanley Haidasz and Alderman Ben Grys.

One of the most devastating emotional reactions happened to two or three Americans and Canadians who went to Rome. The election of the Polish Pope and the whole Roman experience affected them so much that they considered changing their names back to their Polish originals.

They felt so deeply about being Polish. It was a momentous time in history, a mystical and spiritual experience.

What they were trying to say was that no longer need any of us in Canada and the United States be embarrassed that our ancestors were Poles — German Poles, Ukrainian Poles, Jewish Poles, Russian Poles, Czech Poles, Austrian Poles, Lithuanian Poles — the representative of God has come from among us!

11

Senator Stanley Haidasz

Perhaps the most important member of the Canadian delegation to the concelebration in Rome was Senator Stanley Haidasz, MD.

As mentioned previously, he was singled out by name by the Pope. He was at the funeral of Pope Paul VI and he was in the Eternal City to see the elevation of the new Pope. But it was the election of the Polish Pope which underlined the importance of Senator Stanley Haidasz and his role in Canada.

There were 124 foreign delegations in Rome to attend the concelebrated Mass and seven of the delegations were led by their heads of state. Polish President Henryk Jablonski was there, the first Communist head of state ever to attend such a function.

It must be remembered that Senator Haidasz is one of the few of Polish extraction who have become Members of Parliament or members of a legislative assembly in Canada. He was also the first minister of multiculturalism, a new portfolio, and the first senator of Polish extraction. For a while there were rumours that he would become the first Governor General of Polish heritage, but that post fell to Ed Schreyer who is of German background.

Haidasz is the son of Polish immigrants who came to this country in 1911. He was born in Toronto on March 4, 1923. This makes him three years younger than the Pope. Like him, Haidasz has fluency in several languages — English, French, Polish, Ukrainian, Russian. Both the Pope and Haidasz can be expected to live at least another twenty-five years and it is a wonderful asset for Haidasz to have connections with one of the most important offices in the world.

When the beautiful new Canadian embassy building was opened in Warsaw in 1970, Dr. Haidasz was one of the top Canadian representatives. He also accompanied Prime Minister Pierre Trudeau in 1971 on an official visit to the USSR.

When Dr. Haidasz was in Rome for the funeral of Pope Paul VI he had a short conversation with Cardinal Wojtyla along the same vein as previous conversations with the Cardinal on his visits to Canada in 1969 and 1976. The

Cardinal discussed his difficulties with religious instruction, church information and state relations. It required courage, perseverance and tact for Cardinal Wojtyla to deal with the Polish government.

At the same time Cardinal Wojtyla expressed appreciation for the work and accomplishments of Canadians of Polish origin. He also praised the work that Dr. Haidasz was doing as a politician in his stand on human rights.

In an earlier chapter is presented the text of Senator Haidasz's address to the Canadian Senate on the election of the Polish Pope. On behalf of His Holiness, Cardinal Villot, the Vatican secretary of state, sent him a letter thanking him for this moving address.

Dr. Haidasz also received splendid communiqués from Cardinal Wyszynski in Warsaw, Bishop Szczepan Wesoly in Rome and Father Antoni Rabiega of St. Hyacinth's Church in Ottawa.

In 1976, Cardinal Wojtyla renews some old friendships. Here he is shown with Father Grzadziel, Senator Stanley Haidasz and Natalia Haidasz.

12

The Pope and Phenomenology

The last time Cardinal Wojtyla visited the United States of America, in 1976, there were many criticisms from abroad of the United States as a declining power. In a letter-to-the-editor published in a Toronto paper I pointed out that there couldn't be too much wrong with the United States since *all* the Nobel Prizes awarded that year had been won by Americans. This was the first time in history that one country had swept the field.

With this calibre of intellect it is not too surprising that Americans embrace new ideas and philosophies, and even new religions.

One subject which interests many American intellectuals is phenomenology — and Pope John Paul II is an expert in phenomenology. This theory was first expounded by Edmund Husserl in Germany in early 1907. It bases scientific objectivity upon the unique nature of subjective human perception. The Pope has written a major work on this theory, *Person and Act*, which is now being translated into English.

As explained by his translator, Anna-Teresa Tymieniecka, president of the World Institute for Advanced Phenomenological Research and Learning at Belmont, Massachusetts, "He (Wojtyla) stresses the irreducible value of the human person. He finds a spiritual dimension in human interaction, and that leads him to a profoundly humanistic conception of society."

Professor Joseph Kockelmans of Pennsylvania State University believes that some of the Pope's theories on phenomenology will have a lasting impact on the contemporary conception of man.

The American author, Malachi Martin, was a personal assistant to Pope John XXIII and Pope Paul VI and the author of *Three Popes and the Cardinal* and the recent *The Final Conclave*. He observed that as an off-shoot of his study of phenomenology Wojtyla became influenced by Jan Tyrowski, a simple man who had the gift of mystical prayer. He also studied the master of mystical prayer, St. John of the Cross, a Spaniard, and became so engrossed in this study that early in life he too attained this gift.

The gift of mystical prayer helps one to reject all prejudices — every type of human experience and contact is given a legitimate place and a fair hearing.

This is why I believe that this new Pope will be able to speak to any person, to every country, to the entire world with a great degree of humanity. He has already shown this in many episodes of his own life — skiing with his students — lecturing at the university — working with his hands in a quarry — sitting by a camp fire playing his guitar and singing with a crowd — attending a student presentation of "Jesus Christ Super-Star" and enjoying it — delivering a speech from the Vatican in eleven different languages.

As Pontiff I believe that he will talk with the rebels in his church and try to reconcile them, and he will hold dialogue with the Communists. To the women he will give their proper place, for he loves one of them, the Virgin Mary, as much as he loves Christ. He will be pleased to receive a head of state or an archbishop but he will also be happy to see Anthony Quinn. He will admire Michelangelo but he will also get a chuckle out of the cartooning of Andy Donato or Ben Wicks. He will study the Old and New Testaments but he will also delve in and advance phenomenology.

Truly he will be a man for all seasons, for all nations, and for all people.

13

The Pope and Communism

Because the Pope comes from a country which has a Communist government —
and that is different from saying he comes from a Communist country — the
eyes of the world are focused upon him to see how he is going to react to the
spectre which has come out of Eastern Europe and which claims even more
adherents throughout the world than does Catholicism.

After I visited Poland in 1976 I wrote several articles on the Polish church and
Communism for CBC Radio, the *Toronto Star*, the *Catholic Register*, and other

Cardinal Wojtyla amongst the Polish
people in Czestochowa at Jasna Gora.

At Lublin, Poland. Cardinal Wojtyla with Cardinal Krol of Philadelphia and Vice-Minister of Polish Affairs Wieslaw Adamski.

publications. My main thesis was that, ironically, the church was flourishing in "Communist" Poland. Perhaps this was due to the courage and refusal to compromise of Cardinals Wyszynski, Wojtyla and Filipiak. (Cardinal Filipiak died just a few days before the election of Cardinal Wojtyla as Pope.)

With his knowledge of how to exist in a Communist state, indeed, even to flourish for there was a sevenfold increase in churches after World War II — Pope John Paul II may yet convert the Communists, or at least have a splendid détente with them.

Shortly before leaving for Mexico in early 1979 the Pope had an unprecedented meeting with none other than Soviet Foreign Minister Andrei Gromyko. This meeting was more important than any Gromyko had scheduled with top Italian officials. Undoubtedly this encounter foreshadowed developments in the Vatican's future relations with Eastern Europe. Perhaps it will only be a continuation of the "ostpolitik — eastern policy" begun by Pope

Paul VI to ease the conditions of Catholics behind the Iron Curtain. Did this Pope ask for more? No longer can broadcasts be censored as they used to be for now he has the powerful antennae of Vatican Radio to broadcast to Eastern Europe in Polish, Russian, Lithuanian and Ukrainian. Let them try to jam those!

If Stalin were to ask now how many legions the Pope has the reply would be that there are countless legions of Mary and hundreds of millions of people armed with a new morality which will not tolerate tanks.

Since World War II three Hail Marys have been said in some countries of the world for the conversion of Russia after every low Mass in the Catholic church. Now one man has been raised from a Communist state to give power to those three Hail Marys.

God is still far from dead in the USSR.

There are nearly 17,000 congregations in fifty officially recognized religious groups in the Soviet Union. About 100 million people still believe in God. The Russian Orthodox Church has 32 million members. There are still about five million Roman Catholics in the USSR, particularly in Russia and the Ukraine, about half the number there are in Canada. There are many Poles in the Soviet Union, for there are Poles born in the Ukraine and Poles born in Russia.

The Eastern Rite Catholic Church still exists in the USSR. It is one of the seventeen rites of Catholicism, one that many North American Roman Catholics know little about. Most of its adherents are Ukrainians but because the Ukraine is one of the most troubled parts of the USSR these Catholics must practise their faith in an underground manner.

The Soviet Union has its problems with religion, for as well as renascent Catholics there are dissident Jews and militant Moslems.

It is in just such an atmosphere that the Pope can show leadership. After all, during World War II no other church in occupied Europe could equal the Polish church's boldness and defiance of the Nazis.

Similarly, the new Pope and the Polish people can openly defy the Communist government or live in détente with it.

If it is necessary for another Cardinal Wyszynski to go to jail, he will do so — if it is necessary for another Cardinal Wojtyla to break parade rules, he will do so — if it is necessary to invoke Thomistic thought to overcome Marxism, it will be taught.

In all these ideals there is only one leader — His Holiness, Pope John Paul II. He will hold dialogue, he will confront, he will co-exist.

He will bring the world unto peace.

14

The Pope and Feminism

Pope John Paul II holds the absolute admiration and veneration of the Blessed Virgin Mary that is characteristic of most Poles. Woman was chosen by God to bear Him and woman was chosen by God to bear life and continue civilization. Does that bespeak a lesser role?

Yet there are those who have been corrupted by the devious doctrines of the new feminism who imperil the continuation of civilization — if they persist in their beliefs and enlarge their field of action.

Professor Felix Bednarski, professor of Thomistic philosophy in Rome, writes that the Italians have been enthusiastic about the Pope but there are some groups who are attacking his stance on abortion.

The author in front of one of the many wayside shrines to the Blessed Virgin which are found along the highways and byways in Poland.

Why can woman not see that she is a partner with God in the creation of human life, the most sublime manifestation on earth? Everything else is secondary to it.

With abortion, a virtual holocaust is perpetrated annually in this world. Life in its most defenceless state is taken every year in numbers over the six million figure. We cannot blame the Nazis for this holocaust — every country in the world shares in this crime.

I have seen women columnists jeer the Pope's enunciation on motherhood: "Motherhood is a vocation of woman. It was yesterday. It is today. It always will be." But these are not words worthy of contempt — they are among the most sacred ever uttered for women to hear.

Women who reject abortion have been called heroines by Pope John Paul II. But he is a fair man; he will discuss the special problems of pregnant women who are in exceptional circumstances.

The Pope does not want feminists to deflect from their course the women who have cast themselves in the nun's role of chastity, poverty and obedience. And he has urged nuns everywhere to wear distinctly religious garb.

There is much dialogue to be held on such issues as the alarming breakdown of family life through divorce, marriage of the clergy, the possibility of women becoming priests, and the role of women in the church.

The solutions to many problems must be found.

We trust that Pope John Paul II, in his wisdom, will find a way.

15

The First North American Visit — 1969

As president of the Canadian Polish Congress, Zygmunt Jarmicki was the man principally responsible for bringing Cardinal Wojtyla to Canada in 1969. It is because of him that many Canadians had the delight and high honour of meeting the future Pope John Paul II.

Early in 1969 the Canadian Polish Congress sent a letter of invitation to His Eminence, Stefan Cardinal Wyszynski, the Primate of Poland, to visit Canada. Wyszynski was unable to accept the invitation but suggested that Cardinal Wojtyla visit Canada in his place. In his letter of acceptance of June 6 Cardinal Wojtyla wrote, "I consider it very important to establish relations with the Polish community in Canada." This was to be the first visit of a Polish cardinal to Canada.

After Wojtyla accepted the invitation to come to Canada, the committee for the Canadian Polish Congress sent out invitations to Canadian dignitaries to the banquet at the Royal York Hotel in Toronto on September 13. Those invited were His Excellency Roland Michener, the Governor General of Canada, His Eminence, Maurice Cardinal Roy, His Worship Mayor William Dennison, the Hon. John Robarts, Premier of Ontario, the Rt. Hon. Pierre Trudeau, Prime Minister of Canada, His Excellency Emanuele Clarizio, the Apostolic Delegate to Canada. It is interesting to note that only Dennison and Clarizio accepted, although Cardinal Roy was involved in the celebrations in Quebec City.

It is also significant that the RCMP refused the request of J.G. Burski, vice-president of the Canadian Polish Congress, for two uniformed members of the Force to be present for activities involving the Cardinal in Montreal and Toronto.

Detailed arrangements for the Cardinal's tour were made with Bishop Wladyslaw Rubin, the Polish Primate's delegate to Rome who dealt with the affairs of emigrated Poles.

The members of the Congress spent many hours in preparation for the Cardinal's visit and an itinerary of the trip was drawn up by "panie"

Mayor Jean Drapeau and Cardinal Wojtyla exchange gifts and signatures in Montreal in 1969.

In Quebec City, the Primate of Canada, Cardinal Maurice Roy, with Cardinal Wojtyla and Quebec girls in Polish dress.

Berezowska, Bieniasz, Brodzka, Kottowa and "panowie" Ks. Prob. J. Capiga, Burski, Brodzki, Jarmicki, Kogler, Krychowski, Zaremba. A preliminary schedule was prepared by Stanislaw Brodzki.

In his letter of invitation to Cardinal Wyszynski, Jarmicki mentioned that since there were currency difficulties for travellers leaving Poland all expenses for the visit would be borne by the Canadian Polish Congress. He also observed that by coincidence a celebration in honour of St. Hyacinth was to take place in Ottawa during 1969. St. Hyacinth has churches in Warsaw and in Ottawa. The celebrations in Ottawa were to mark the seven hundred and fiftieth anniversary of St. Hyacinth's pilgrimage from Krakow to Rome. Relics of St. Hyacinth were sent from Poland to Ottawa and their arrival was timed to coincide with the anniversary celebrations and the visit of Cardinal Wojtyla.

Cardinal Wojtyla and his party arrived in Montreal on August 28 and were greeted at the airport by Zygmunt Jarmicki and members of the Canadian Polish Congress. On August 29 they met the Archbishop of Montreal, Paul Grègoire, and were officially welcomed to the city by Mayor Jean Drapeau.

In Montreal, as in every other city on his tour, Cardinal Wojtyla was joyously received by enthusiastic crowds when he made his public appearances. Of course the Polish citizens of each community claimed him as their own and he was greeted in every city by young people in Polish costume bearing flowers and gifts.

Cardinal Maurice Roy, himself once *papabile*, with Cardinal Wojtyla in Quebec City in 1969.

Official welcome to Quebec City, August, 1969.

On August 30 the Cardinal and his party travelled to Quebec City where they were welcomed by Maurice Cardinal Roy, the Primate of Canada.

On September 1 Cardinal Wojtyla arrived in Ottawa and met with the Apostolic Delegate, Emanuele Clarizio. The next day he attended the anniversary celebrations at St. Hyacinth's Church and presented to Reverend Rabiega the sacred relics of St. Hyacinth.

Then the party from Poland and their Canadian hosts flew from Ottawa to Edmonton and were received there by Archbishop A. Jordan and S. Wachowicz. On the following day they visited Polonia in Calgary and the mountaineer Wojtyla was taken to Banff where he marvelled at the Canadian Rockies.

The party returned to Edmonton and from there they flew to Winnipeg on September 6 to be met by Cardinal George Flahiff and Jozef Kucharzyk.

On September 8 Cardinal Wojtyla arrived in Toronto and was taken to the Oblate Fathers' Retreat House in Port Credit. The next morning he arrived in Toronto to be met by Archbishop Philip Pocock, Mayor William Dennison, and Aldermen Fred Beavis, Margaret Campbell and Ben Grys.

The Cardinal went to Hamilton on September 10 to meet Bishop Joseph Ryan. The following day he met Bishop Emmett Carter in London and a lasting friendship was formed with the man who today is Archbishop of Toronto. I think the Archbishop captured the Cardinal's heart when he held a little ceremony for the Madonna of Czestochowa who is held in special veneration by the Pope.

On September 12 the Cardinal was back in Toronto where he visited the Polish parishes and great celebrations were held in his honour. Bishop Thomas McCarthy received him in St. Catharines on September 15 and the following day he concluded his tour of Canada with a visit to Niagara Falls.

Then Cardinal Wojtyla crossed over the Peace Bridge to Buffalo and embarked on his first visit to the United States of America.

Cardinal Wojtyla has tea in the home of Zygmunt Jarmicki in Toronto, 1969.

16

Cardinal Wojtyla's Visit to Montreal

Montreal is the city which played host to the world showcase, Expo 67, and to the Olympic Games in 1976. So of course Cardinal Wojtyla had to visit Montreal and to meet its mayor, one of the great citizens of the world, Jean Drapeau, who engineered both of these feats.

The inimitable, friendly Jean Drapeau told me over long-distance telephone: "But when he became Pope I didn't know it was the man whom I had received at City Hall in Montreal in 1969. It was my daughter-in-law who phoned me to tell me that the Polish Pope was the man who visited Montreal in 1969. She should remember because when Cardinal Wojtyla visited Montreal in 1969 and was presented to me as the Polish cardinal I told him I had a daughter-in-law who

Mayor Jean Drapeau of Montreal asks His Eminence to speak to his daughter-in-law on long-distance telephone. Both photographs show characteristic hand poses.

The famed Black Madonna of Czestochowa.

On the site of the exhibition, *Man and His World*, in Montreal. In the background, the statue of Copernicus, the Polish founder of modern astronomy.

The Choir of St. Stanislaus' Church, Toronto, with Cardinal Wojtyla in September, 1969.

The Cardinal meets Dr. Wojciech Gregorowicz.

Welcome at Toronto City Hall, September 1969.

Mayor William Dennison of Toronto and Alderman Ben Grys greet Cardinal Wojtyla and Bishops Wesoly. Father Z. Peszkowski is in the background.

Cardinal Wojtyla and Bishop Wesoly with Alderman Margaret Campbell.

Rudolf Kogler (right), who attended school with Karol Wojtyla in Poland for eight years, looks pleased as Alderman Fred Beavis shows the Cardinal the Toronto Book. Father MacKarski and Alderman Ben Grys look on.

Cardinal Wojtyla and the Apostolic Pro-Nuncio, His Grace Archbishop Angelo Palmas, with Zygmunt Jarmicki.

John Yaremko, an Ontario cabinet minister who toured Poland in 1976, meets His Eminence in Toronto.

Stanley Haidasz, M.P. and his wife Natalia meet Cardinal Wojtyla. Haidasz later became Minister for Multiculturalism in the Trudeau government and then a Senator.

Luncheon in Niagara Falls at the Montrose Motor Inn, with Ted Stelmaszynski, Very Reverend M. Clifford, Mayor F. Miller and Father J. Klita.

Mass at the Coliseum, Canadian National Exhibition, September, 1969.

A dinner in Toronto, 1976, with Rudolf Kogler, Senator Stanley Haidasz and Judge Irena Unger.

Tadeusz Gonsik presents a gift to Cardinal Wojtyla, at the St. Stanislaus Parish Credit Union Hall, 1976.

Bishop Wladislaw Rubin, in charge of Polish emigrants throughout the world, with Cardinal Wojtyla.

Celebrating Mass in St. Michael's Cathedral, Toronto, August, 1976.

Pope John Paul II in Rome with his new Cross.

On December 14, 1978, His Holiness presented a rosary to His Grace, Archbishop Gerald Emmett Carter of Toronto. Archbishop Carter's credentials are on the plate.

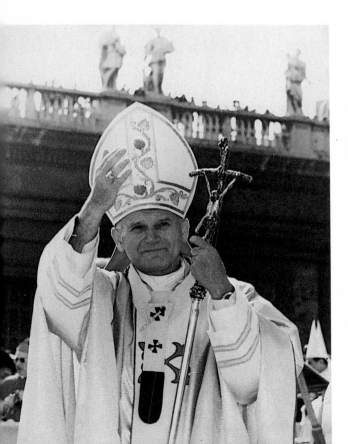

His Holiness in Rome, with Cardinal Wyszynski.

Pope John Paul II in Rome at one of the first audiences after his election.

was Polish who was honeymooning in Miami. On inspiration (Drapeau has the greatest ideas in the world) I asked him if he would like to speak to my daughter-in-law in Polish. So I called her long distance in Miami and he carried on a conversation with her right from my office!"

While in Montreal Cardinal Wojtyla said Mass with Paul Grègoire, Archbishop of Montreal. When the Archbishop was in Rome after the election of Pope John Paul II he said, "The fact that the new Pope is not Italian expresses the universal dimension of the Church. He makes the bridge between East and West."

There was one man in Montreal who was caught up with the Pope as much as I was during the Christmas season of 1978. Both of us had our personal Christmas cards made up with a photograph of Pope John Paul II. Later I was to learn that Father Capiga of Hamilton also did this. Casimir Stanczykowski, who started multicultural radio in Montreal, had a Christmas card showing the Pope with messages in English, French and Polish.

Both he and Johnny Lombardi, who started multicultural radio in Toronto, are of Polish and Italian heritage and they were both invited to the papal funerals and installations held during the latter part of 1978. The Cardinal's visits of 1969 and 1976 were extensively reported on Stanczykowski's CFMB of Montreal and Lombardi's CHIN radio of Toronto which illustrates that multicultural radio can be very effective in interpreting news of world importance to the people most concerned.

His Holiness in Montreal in 1969 as Cardinal Wojtyla, with Casimir Stanczykowski, President of radio station CFMB, a multicultural station which suited the multilingual new Pope.

The Cardinal visited Man and His World, the permanent exhibit at the site of Expo 67, with Eugene Baranowski, chairman of the Montreal Branch of the Canadian Polish Congress. There is a large Polish population in Montreal and the Cardinal was joyfully received by members of the Polish community. A stirring programme of folk dances was presented by youthful dancers in native Polish costume.

There is a priest in Montreal, Reverend Simon Grodski, pastor of Our Lady of Czestochowa in the east end, who also recalled Cardinal Wojtyla's visit. Grodski knew Cardinal Wojtyla in Poland before he immigrated to Canada in 1967. He thinks the Pope can talk to anyone and can communicate especially well with young people. He was often to be found in "rap" sessions with the young at the University of Krakow, Grodski said, and he could even talk with the Communist authorities with openness. It is Grodski's opinion that the election of Cardinal Wojtyla as Pope will help relations between church and state in Poland because the government has always wanted a concordat with the Vatican.

17

The Ottawa Visit

The nation's capital of Ottawa numbers about five thousand in its Polish community. Among them is the sister of the Prime Minister who is married to a Pole. There is also the new ambassador, Dr. Stanislaw Pawlak. Sitting in the ranks of the Opposition in the House of Commons is Steve Paproski of Edmonton.

Probably the person in Ottawa who was most elated about the election of Pope John Paul II was Father Antoni Rabiega of the Polish parish of St. Hyacinth which Cardinal Wojtyla visited in 1969. Father Rabiega said, "The new Pope came and we celebrated all day. In the evening everyone was on stage singing a typical Polish song. We were very happy."

Mira Gawalewicz, president of the Canadian Polish Congress in Ottawa, told a reporter from the *Ottawa Citizen* that the new Pope would aid the cause of religious freedom, not only in Poland, but in all countries in which Catholics face repressive political regimes.

Ottawa's Roman Catholic Archbishop, Joseph-Aurèle Plourde, with whom the Cardinal stayed in 1969, said, "With the expansion of Communism throughout the world he may be just the man we need."

On the lighter side is the tale of a teenage boy who was just six years old in 1969 who will also never forget the Cardinal's visit to Ottawa. Stepping out from the crowd, his finger in his mouth, he shyly offered the Cardinal a picture to autograph. The Cardinal signed it graciously and quipped, "But if I put my finger in my mouth I may give you a bad example."

Policeman Denis Lacroix tells of sternly raising his hand and loudly blowing his whistle to halt a limousine making a wrong turn on an Ottawa street, and describes his embarrassment and dismay on discovering that it was carrying Cardinal Wojtyla.

Dr. Victor Szyrynski, professor of psychiatry at the University of Ottawa, was one person who always believed in the eventual ascendancy of Cardinal Wojtyla to the papacy. In 1974 Dr. Szyrynski arranged for his daughter to be married by Cardinal Wojtyla in his private chapel in Krakow. Zygmunt Jarmicki's daughter

Cardinal Wojtyla meets with members of the Polish community at a reception in Ottawa.

Zuni was present at this ceremony and Cardinal Wojtyla recognized her and remembered her from his visit to her home in Toronto in 1969.

Another Ottawa churchman who is a friend of the Pope is Father Guy Poisson. With Archbishop G. Emmett Carter of Toronto he made a visit to Cardinal Wojtyla in Krakow. Father Poisson recalls an example of his humour: "A Polish jet buzzed an outdoor ceremony and the Cardinal interjected, 'Even heaven is coming to present its greetings to our Canadian visitors.' "

18

Cardinal Wojtyla
Visits Western Canada

There are just as many people of Polish descent in western Canada as there are in Quebec and Ontario. In 1969 Cardinal Wojtyla visited the western cities as the Polish cardinal but if he were to visit any city in Canada or the United States now he would come as the Supreme Pontiff with all Catholics nearly as proud of him as the Poles are.

As an example, Archbishop Joseph MacNeil of Winnipeg said of the new Pope, "He brings an outlook we have not had in more than four hundred years. But his election was inevitable. After all, only twenty-six of the present one hundred and eleven cardinals are Italian, and this had to happen sooner or later."

It was Zygmunt Jarmicki, as president of the Canadian Polish Congress, who first brought Cardinal Wojtyla to Canada in 1969 and thus put this "Canadian claim and stamp" on him.

Cardinal Wojtyla flew from Ottawa to Edmonton and then on to Calgary. On his arrival in Calgary he was presented with the wide-brimmed Stetson hat which is traditionally given to official guests of that city. "Immediately Cardinal Wojtyla donned his at the airport and wore it with a smile. We all received a hat and I have mine to this day," said Jarmicki.

The episode of the Stetson hat continued right through until 1978. After his election as Pope John Paul II, some Calgary people heard that the Stetson given to him in 1969 had been damaged so through Judd Schumiatcher they donated a new one made partially of fur which was delivered to the Vatican with the help of CP Air.

Because Cardinal Wojtyla was known to be a mountaineer and skier, his Calgary hosts took him to Banff to see the Canadian Rockies. He marvelled at the mountains and said they reminded him of the Carpathians around Zakopane not far from Krakow and his home town of Wadowice.

The Polish party flew from Banff to Edmonton in a private plane under bad flying conditions, but this didn't upset the Cardinal at all. From there they flew to Winnipeg where they were received by Cardinal Flahiff. The City of Winnipeg

Cardinal Wojtyla at a reception in his honour in Calgary, Alberta. To a Pole, to receive flowers from a young girl is an expression of prayer.

made Cardinal Wojtyla an honorary citizen. At a dinner he addressed six hundred and fifty members of the Polish community of Manitoba. Then lawyer Ken Galenchuk presented him with a plaque proclaiming the honorary citizenship. Galenchuk remembers that the Cardinal "had a princely presence."

In 1969 there were no Polish organizations in Saskatchewan so Cardinal Wojtyla did not visit that province. But if he should come again to Canada, this time as the Pope, the organizations of the Catholic churches in all the provinces will be pleased and eager to greet him. It won't be just little communities like Krakow in Alberta, Kuroki in Saskatchewan, Jaroslaw in Manitoba, or Warsaw in Ontario that will be ready to receive him; he will be joyously awaited at the Olympic Stadium in Montreal, Maple Leaf Gardens in Toronto, the Coliseum in Edmonton and the Coliseum in Vancouver.

There are more than twenty Polish Roman Catholic churches in Manitoba, over seventeen in Saskatchewan, over seventeen in Alberta, more than twenty-two in Ontario and four in Quebec, two in British Columbia and one in Nova Scotia. There are also at least seven Polish National Catholic churches in Canada. In the Polish Roman Catholic churches the dominant language is English, even though most of the priests are Polish.

Saskatchewan was not included in the 1969 visit but there is a priest in Zenon Park, Saskatchewan, Monsignor Edmund Ulinski, who has known Pope John Paul II since 1962. Monsignor Ulinski came to Canada in 1969 and he thinks that the election as Pope of an archbishop from a Communist country has special meaning.

And it is I, a Saskatchewan-born man, who wrote this book.

19

Visits in the Toronto Area

Undoubtedly Toronto was the focal point of Cardinal Wojtyla's visit to North America in 1969. The Canadian Polish Congress, which was celebrating its twenty-fifth anniversary, first invited the Cardinal to visit Toronto. When confirmation was received that he could come, the tour for the rest of the country was planned. Subsequently the Americans invited him to the United States. Both countries profited greatly as the tour became very extensive indeed and laid the groundwork of the magnificent rapport we Canadians and Americans have with Pope John Paul II.

On September 8, Cardinal Wojtyla was met at the Toronto airport by a welcoming party and taken to the Oblate Fathers' Retreat House at Port Credit which became the headquarters for his Ontario visit. On the morning of September 9 he visited Archbishop Philip Pocock of Toronto and celebrated with him a triumphant Mass in St. Michael's Cathedral. He then returned to Port Credit to meet members of the Polish community.

Next day he went to Hamilton to visit and from there on to London where he stayed with Bishop Emmett Carter, now Archbishop of Toronto. On September 12 he was back in Toronto and that evening he visited the Canadian Legion Hall

The Cardinal and his party arrive at Toronto International Airport in 1969.

Talking with author Benedykt Heydenkorn at the Canadian Legion Hall.

At Toronto City Hall with Alderman Fred Beavis, later the first Roman Catholic mayor of Toronto, and Alderman Ben Grys.

on Dovercourt Avenue to meet Polish veterans, young people and prominent citizens, and to enjoy a festive banquet.

On the evening of September 13 he was at the Royal York Hotel where the Poles took over the Concert Hall to mark the twenty-fifth anniversary celebrations of the Canadian Polish Congress.

On September 14 the Coliseum at the Canadian National Exhibition, which seats 7,500 people, was the scene of a giant religious gathering in which the Cardinal concelebrated Mass. Present on the makeshift altar was a very large portrait of the Madonna of Czestochowa.

In 1976 the Cardinal visited Toronto once again. It was Father Joseph Capiga who was instrumental in bringing him to Hamilton in 1976 but Tadeusz Gonsik, president of the St. Stanislaus and St. Casimir Parish Credit Union Limited of Toronto, wrote many letters to the Cardinal and to Bishop Rubin in Rome to see if he would come again to Toronto after the Eucharistic Congress in Philadelphia.

With the co-operation of Father Michael Smith of the Oblate Fathers, Mr. Gonsik invited Cardinal Wojtyla and seventeen Polish bishops and priests to visit

Cardinal Wojtyla in 1976 with Tadeusz Gonsik, president of the St. Stanislaus Parish Credit Union Limited, the man who was most responsible for bringing the Polish Cardinal to Toronto for the second time.

the Credit Union Hall to meet its members, to concelebrate a Mass at St. Michael's Cathedral, and to rest at the Oblate Fathers' Retreat House in Mississauga.

As the photographs taken at the Credit Union Hall and in St. Michael's Cathedral show, the informal days in Toronto were greatly enjoyed and provided a much needed break for the party from Poland.

The Cardinal renewed his acquaintance with Stanley Haidasz, MP, and with Benedykt Heydenkorn, author and journalist, who is connected with the *Polish Alliancer*.

Mr. Gonsik received from Cardinal Wojtyla a plaque, a white eagle, and statue of the Madonna. His gift in return on behalf of the committee was a set of Olympic silver coins.

Mr. Gonsik also had the happy experience of going to Rome for the

At the St. Stanislaus Parish Credit Union Hall, in Toronto in 1976. *Left* — An exchange of gifts with Wladislaw Gertler and Stanislaw Brodski. *Right* — The Cardinal meets some boys and girls in Polish costume.

installation of Pope John Paul II. While in Rome, he was part of a group of forty-eight people who were received in a private audience. The group was composed of presidents of Catholic organizations from several parts of the world.

Karol Cardinal Wojtyla celebrates Mass in St. Michael's Cathedral, Toronto.

In 1969, Cardinal Wojtyla visited Oshawa's St. Hedwig's Church with Bishop Wesoly of the Polish pastoral centre in Rome. They are shown with Reverend Anthony Bagsik (right), the previous pastor of St. Hedwig's, and the late Msgr. Paul Dwyer.

Undoubtedly Pope John Paul II has a great fondness for Toronto. Surely we shall see him here again sometime in the future.

It was a great day for the Polish people of Oshawa, the Detroit of Canada, when Cardinal Wojtyla visited in 1969, and now that day holds even more significance.

The Cardinal visited St. Hedwig's Church with Bishop Szczepan Wesoly. In our Oshawa picture they are shown with Reverend Anthony Bagsik and the late Monsignor Paul Dwyer. This photograph was personally delivered to me by Terry Kelly, QC, a prominent Oshawa lawyer, who was greatly impressed by the significance of the occasion.

Hank Kolodziejczak, an *Oshawa Times* staff writer and reporter, has the hobby of writing to influential people in the world. He has written to Pierre Trudeau, Menachem Begin (a former Pole) and Jimmy Carter. Cardinal Wojtyla's election as Pope presented him with the opportunity for his greatest coup.

Kolodziejczak sent a cablegram to the new Pope immediately upon hearing of his election. This was answered by Cardinal Villot, the secretary of state, now dead, with a blessing from the Pope.

Three weeks later, still flushed with excitement about the thrilling addition to his collection, Hank telephoned the Vatican. He was told that never in history had the Holy See received so many telegrams and letters. New staff had to be hired just to answer mail.

The new Pope was the world's latest celebrity!

20

The Faithful of Hamilton

No one in Hamilton seemed more pleased with the election of the Polish Pope than Bishop Joseph F. Ryan who headed the Roman Catholic diocese of Hamilton from 1937 to 1973. During this period a large number of European Catholics came to Hamilton, which is known as the Pittsburgh of Canada, and took arduous jobs in the steel mills.

In the new Pope Bishop Ryan found a leader who shares many of his own deep concerns, such as disturbing new attitudes in society, sexual immorality both in real life and as depicted on television, hedonism, and exaggerated demands for freedom which no one knows how to handle. Bishop Ryan is alarmed by the growing divorce rate, the increase in the number of abortions, and the general deterioration of family life. Bishop Ryan is now eighty-one and has retired from his diocese which numbers over two hundred and fifty

Cardinal Wojtyla in Hamilton, Ontario, in 1969. He understood the workingman's city of Hamilton, for he too had worked in a chemical plant when he was a young man during World War II.

thousand people and has one hundred and seventeen parishes. He still treasures his photograph taken with Cardinal Wojtyla in 1969 and is gratified that the new pontiff endures the same anxieties. Bishop Ryan has always been especially interested in Catholic education. He is convinced that it encourages sound moral values and inclines one to do the right thing in life despite all temptations.

Father Joseph Capiga of Hamilton, who was the first to invite Cardinal Wojtyla to Canada in 1976, was in Amsterdam on his way to Poland when he heard the joyful news that the Cardinal had been elected as Pope. He immediately changed his plans and flew to Rome. Pope John Paul II spotted him among the crowd and called out, "Hello, Joe Hamilton!"

Bishop Paul Redding of Hamilton recalled that Cardinal Wojtyla had an hour's conversation with him in 1976 and that the Cardinal visited the Cathedral of Christ the King and St. Stanislaus parish, and stayed three nights in the Mount Cenacle Retreat House. Bishop Redding relates that he discussed Polish topics with the Cardinal in 1976 but he also said, "I don't look upon the Holy Father as being Italian or Polish or whatever. He is the Vicar of Christ on earth; that is the essential quality."

It takes a woman to be enthusiastic and Sister Rita of Hamilton was certainly all of that when the new Pope was elected. As Cardinal Wojtyla he had signed the register at Mount Cenacle Retreat House on August 18, 19, and 20, 1976. She said, "We still have the picture of Our Lady of Poland, the Blessed Mother of God, which he left with us. It was put away but now we will display it. Pope John Paul is a man who will understand the whole world."

The sisters had prepared Polish dishes for the Cardinal's party. Father Capiga's cook, Josephine Kapuscinski, came over to supervise the cooking.

Father Zygmunt Baranoski of St. Margaret Mary Church in Hamilton possibly foresaw greatness — he was one of the few people in Hamilton who asked for Cardinal Wojtyla's autograph when he visited Hamilton in 1976. When asked about the Cardinal he said, "Like every Pole his religious inclination to God is through Mary. Therefore I think the Blessed Mother will lead him and give him advice." (A Catholic may not worship Mary, although there are some who would raise Mary to become co-redemptrix of the world. Some Catholics believe not only in the guidance of the Holy Spirit but also in Mary's. It should please the new feminists that a woman should take her place with a man as redeemers of the world.) Father Baranoski also admits that he prayed that the new Pope would be Polish.

Father Leonard Krsywda, pastor of St. Stanislaus parish in Hamilton, was born in Chicago of Polish parents. He spoke like the Americans who are better

Outside the Cathedral of Christ the King, Hamilton, in 1976.

versed in the devilments of Communism than are Canadians when he said, ''It will now be much more difficult for the Polish government and the other governments behind the Iron Curtain to explain away whatever injustices they have perpetrated.''

The church in Hamilton is keeping abreast of current world issues. Bishop Redding told Charles Wilkinson, religion editor of the *Hamilton Spectator*, that in his *ad limina* visit to Rome he would be discussing the charismatic movement, the Cursillo movement, marriage encounter, women's movements, and the need for the clergy to deal with social consequences arising from increasing numbers of immigrants from other cultures.

Since the election of Pope John Paul II two Catholic leaders, one from the laity and one from the church, have arrived in Hamilton with news from Rome. Roman Catholic affairs receive very good press coverage in Hamilton — it has been observed that the present Pope is receiving more attention than the previous four popes put together.

Andrew Wielowieyski is the general secretary of the Club of Catholic Intellectuals in Warsaw which has two thousand members. He has also skied with Cardinal Wojtyla. He visited McMaster University a short while ago where he made the following comment: ''The election of Wojtyla is the victory of

68

A happy moment shared in the Cathedral of Christ the King, Hamilton.

Cardinal Wyszynski's life. He has been Primate of Poland for over thirty years and without his cleverness and strength it would not have been possible for Cardinal Wojtyla to have such prestige in the church."

Father Tadeusz Kaszuba, superior general of the Congregation of the Resurrection in Rome, also visited Hamilton recently. He remarked that there will now be a different orientation to the church. He thinks the new Pope will travel a great deal and he told of the trips that had already been scheduled to Mexico and Poland in 1979. The Pope may even come to Canada. Father Kaszuba also expects that he will visit shrines such as Fatima in Portugal because he has tremendous devotion to the Blessed Virgin. (The Pope's new coat of arms has a large *M* for Mary emblazoned on the shield.) Father Kaszuba mentioned as well the Pope's tremendous powers of concentration. "As a university professor he would speak for four hours nonstop, break for ten minutes, and then continue for another two hours."

Just what did Cardinal Wojtyla do when he was in Hamilton in 1969 to make such a lasting impression on its Catholic citizens? He dined with twenty Polish clergymen, officiated at a benediction where he met parishioners, and then went to the Polish Alliance hall to meet Polish children who staged a programme for him. Later he greeted Polish veterans from both world wars.

A former president of the Hamilton Branch of the Canadian Polish Congress, Mr. Leonard Jurkowski, has met the Pope twice. He wrote me a letter and included a magnificent tribute by S.M. Hudecki, MD, FRCS(C), on the occasion of the installation of Pope John Paul II.

Dr. Hudecki related that he went to Rome for the ceremony because he had an overwhelming desire to take part in this historical event — he knew that the Polish Pope would be ranked in Poland with such legendary figures as

The Cardinal speaks at a reception in the Parish Hall of St. Stanislaus' Church in Hamilton, Ontario.

Copernicus and Chopin. The doctor from Hamilton observed that this most accessible Pope yearned to be close to the people. He said that his voice was a booming baritone and he changed from one language to another with disarming ease.

In a moving paragraph, Dr. Hudecki wrote: "I personally was moved emotionally on the day following the installation when some seven thousand Poles met with their Cardinal and Bishops at a special audience to bid farewell to the Pope. The spokesman for the Polish people was their Primate, Cardinal Wyszynski. The farewell address culminated with the seventy-seven-year-old Cardinal on his knees kissing the ring of the Pope, then the latter vigorously knelt beside him and embraced him. Both were on their knees and in tears. The crowd responded first with unbelieving silence, punctuated with sobs, and moments later burst into songs of their homeland."

At the height of this moment of mass spiritual exaltation, the crowd fully sensed that the Pope was intimating that it was the faith of the people of Poland through a thousand years of travail and oppression that had prepared him for the role which had been so precipitously thrust upon him.

70

You can imagine the scene and how the Hamilton delegation responded! As well as Dr. and Mrs. Hudecki, the Hamilton party included Father Chester Chmurzynski, Father Joseph Kamienski, Helga Murray, Helen Gura, Litka Korbut, Irene Fialkowski, Ann Brodowski, Josephine Kapuscinski, and Mrs. Pauline Kostiuk. For each one there could be no more memorable sight in a lifetime.

21

Cardinal Wojtyla Visits
St. Catharines and Niagara Falls

The Polish people of St. Catharines, Ontario well remember when Cardinal Wojtyla visited on September 15, 1969. He was welcomed at the city hall, said Mass at Our Lady of Perpetual Help Church and attended a banquet. This year these people are preparing to celebrate the fiftieth anniversary of the Polish Society — and now they have a Polish Pope!

Jack Gatecliff, sports editor of the *St. Catharines Standard*, quotes Father Felix Kwiatkowski as saying that the election of a Polish Pope signifies that the Polish people are reaping the blessings of God for their years of continuous struggle, for their faith which never wavered despite their great suffering during the Second World War. This suffering seems to parallel the holocaust suffered by the Jews. Both the Poles and the Jews, many of whom were Poles, have been rewarded. The Jews have their new state of Israel and the rest of the Poles have their Pope!

In 1969 Leon Ananicz of St. Catharines was kissed on the cheek by Cardinal Wojtyla after presenting his gift. John Bucko laid a wreath with the Cardinal at Niagara-on-the-Lake in honour of the Polish war dead.

Just like any tourist, particularly one from an Eastern European country, Cardinal Wojtyla really wanted to see Niagara Falls when he came to Canada.

Ted Stelmaszynski, general manager of the Montrose Motor Inn in Niagara Falls, has most pleasant recollections of the Cardinal's visit. "He stayed in the Montrose Motor Inn," he told me by telephone. Just like those signs in the United States which read "George Washington Slept Here," maybe Ted should put one up which says "Pope John Paul II Slept Here." Prior to the Cardinal's visit, Ted's most famous guests were hockey players who attended the wedding of Toronto Maple Leaf Rick Ley. At the wedding were Ron Ellis, George Armstrong, Tim Horton, Marcel Pronovost, and Mike Pelyk who left Ted an autographed hockey stick which he has in his family "museum." I imagine the hockey stick will now take second place to the postcard Ted received from Cardinal Wojtyla. When I saw this card it was the first time that I had seen the signature "Karol Kard. Wojtyla" and it sent shivers up my back.

KAROL KARDYNAŁ WOJTYŁA   Kraków - Boże Narodzenie 1969.
ARCYBISKUP METROPOLITA KRAKOWSKI

Szanowni i Drodzy Państwo,

Za życzenia świąteczno-nowo-
roczne uprzejmie dziękuję i od-
powiadam takimi samymi życzenia-
mi życząc łaski Bożego Narodzenia
dla całej Rodziny.
Łączę jeszcze raz wyrazy
szczerej wdzięczności i należnego
szacunku

BÓG SIĘ RODZI

+ Karol kard. Wojtyła

Kp. 1733 67 — 5000 — R-54(177)

A card of greeting received from Karol Cardinal Wojtyla by Ted Stelmaszynski,
General Manager of the Montrose Motor Inn in Niagara Falls, Ontario.

Ted relates that a group which gathered for luncheon in Niagara Falls
presented the Cardinal with a very expensive bottle of cognac. "Showing both
his humour and his restraint at once," says Ted, "the Cardinal said in acceptance
that a pair of shoes would have been appreciated more.

"When he stayed in our Room Eight we found him a very charming man. He
didn't drink the cognac but we had coffee and hot chocolate with him." Using
language of the mountainous region of Poland, Ted described the new Pope as
"a herdsman."

A visit to the Skylon Tower in Niagara Falls, Ontario,
with Bishop Wesoly and Bishop Thomas McCarthy.

The Cardinal in joyful conversation with a Polish parishioner at Niagara Falls, Ontario.

Ted Stelmaszynski knows now that Pope John Paul II is the most important person who has ever stayed with him and he has quickly assembled his mementoes of the 1969 visit. One is a small wooden box used to store pens and pencils which was a gift to him from the Cardinal. He also treasures memories of a visit he made to Krakow where he once again met and dined with Cardinal Wojtyla.

Tony Fredo, director of public relations for Ford of Canada at Oakville, was once a reporter for the *Niagara Falls Review*, and he sent me some material about the Polish Pontiff.

One of the references was to Emilia Hofmann of Niagara Falls who danced in her kitchen when she heard of the election of Cardinal Wojtyla. She had been taught religion by him at Saint Szczepan Church in Krakow when she was a child. She now cherishes even more the certificates she received as a child which had been signed by Father Wojtyla. To be taught catechism by a priest who would one day become Pope is indeed awe inspiring! Mrs. Hofmann also disclosed that some children went secretly to Father Wojtyla's classes — under the rule of Stalin if they had been found out it would have meant the end of their fathers' jobs.

When Bishop Thomas Fulton of St. Catharines was in Rome in mid-November 1978, the Pope spoke to some thirty-five Canadian bishops and he recalled his visit to St. Catharines and Niagara Falls. The Pope spoke to the Canadians in English and in French and asked them to take his paternal benediction to all the people of Canada.

22

Cardinal Wojtyla's Visit to the United States in 1969

The head of the special committee which organized Cardinal Wojtyla's 1969 visit to the United States was Most Reverend Alfred Abramowicz, the auxiliary bishop of Chicago. The Reverend Walter J. Ziemba of Orchard Lake, Michigan, was his co-chairman and he made many of the detailed preparations. During his visit the Cardinal was accompanied by Bishop Szczepan Wesoly of the Polish pastoral centre in Rome and by Bishop W. Rubin who is in charge of the pastoral care of Polish immigrants in all parts of the world.

With a great flourish, the special committee sent out publicity releases to the Polish press and radio stations throughout the country and to many of the English-speaking Catholic newspapers. After all, Americans of Polish descent equal about half the entire population of Canada!

In a finely worded publicity release it was announced that the Cardinal would travel to fourteen different cities to thank American Poles for the great assistance they had rendered to the church in Poland during some of the most critical years in its history. The American hosts also considered the Cardinal's visit to be a golden opportunity for American Polonia to make citizens of the United States aware of Poland and of the heroism of its church. The fourteen cities to be visited were Buffalo, Hartford, Cleveland, Pittsburgh, Detroit, Orchard Lake, Boston, Washington, Baltimore, St. Louis, Chicago, Philadelphia, Doylestown and New York.

Chicago has a Polish population greater than Warsaw's. An even bigger concentration of native Poles in North America, if you include Jews born in Poland who are generally not included in tabulations like this, is in New York City.

As soon as Cardinal Wojtyla arrived in Buffalo on September 16, 1969, a press conference was held for him in typical American fashion. Then a Mass was said at St. Stanislaus Church. The next day the Cardinal attended a civic reception given by the mayor of Buffalo at the Hotel Statler.

The party flew from Buffalo to Hartford, Connecticut where again a press conference and a reception were held. Then on to Cleveland where the Cardinal was received by Monsignor E.J. Modzelewski and a dinner was held at Cavoli's. In Pittsburgh the Cardinal went to the residence of Bishop Leonard for lunch. The following day there was a procession to the cathedral where Mass was said. This was followed by the dedication of a plaque at the Madame Marie Curie Sklodowska Science Building at the University of Pittsburgh.

On September 22 the party arrived in Detroit and had lunch at Cardinal Dearden's home. Cardinal Wojtyla stayed overnight at Orchard Lake where he placed a memorial wreath on the grave of Father Dabrowski in Mt. Elliott Cemetery.

Flying back east to Boston, the Cardinal was greeted in Boston on September 24 by Monsignor Sypek and he later attended a dinner given by Cardinal Cushing, the Kennedys' favourite cardinal.

In Washington, Cardinal Wojtyla was received by Cardinal O'Boyle. There were several cardinals and bishops in attendance at a reception there for him and as well Senator Edmund Muskie, the highest-ranking political figure of Polish ancestry in the United States prior to Zbigniew Brzezinski.

Cardinal Carberry welcomed Cardinal Wojtyla in St. Louis on September 26. Then he journeyed on to Chicago where there was a dedication of a Millenium Shrine and also a dedication at St. Hyacinth's Church (so one more St. Hyacinth Church had been found!)

On September 28 the party arrived in Philadelphia where they were met by Cardinal John Krol who is of Polish descent. Cardinal Krol and Cardinal Wojtyla travelled by helicopter to Doylestown from Philadelphia to see the monastery there.

Cardinal Wojtyla arrived in New York on September 29 where he was greeted by Father Fus. The Cardinal stayed at the Waldorf Astoria and attended a reception given by Cardinal Cooke. He also concelebrated Mass at St. Patrick's Cathedral.

On September 30 the Cardinal and his party flew from New York to Rome. Their departure was saluted with a "Z Bogiem!"

23

How the People of Buffalo Felt

There are some 350,000 Americans in Buffalo of Polish background — this is about the size of the entire Polish community in Canada. You can imagine how ecstatic these people were when Cardinal Wojtyla was elected Pope! The *Buffalo Evening News* and the *Courier Express* had headlines and sections as big as when the American president, McKinley, was assassinated in their city in 1901. There were special editions and special reports. There was a full-page picture in colour of Pope John Paul II and Buffalo Bishop Edward D. Head after the investiture in Rome.

Edward L. Kasprzak, the Buffalo photographer who has supplied some of the pictures for this book, had a field day. Papers ran dozens of his photos from the 1969 and 1976 visits. One couple who owned a sausage company ordered five hundred prints of the Pope and gave them away to customers. Another restaurateur gave away a print of the Pope every time a meal was served. Christmas cards showing the Pope were quickly made up for the 1978 season and one Buffalo company issued a calendar featuring the new Pope.

There was supreme joy in Buffalo.

What was manifest in Buffalo and in the other cities of North America was that this Pope was actually known by so many of the people. He was not a distant trans-Atlantic Pope, a foreigner, or a mystical figure of someone's religious imagination. There were many people who had had a cup of tea with him and some who had drunk a beer with him. Others had shared a joke with him. There

In 1969, the Cardinal visited Buffalo and met (left to right) Joseph Starosciak, Mr. and Mrs. Edward Poluszny, Mrs. Genevieve Starosciak, Auxiliary Bishop Stanislaus Brzana, and Monsignor Kazmierczak.

In Buffalo, the Cardinal met many children from the Polish Catholic community.

is no other ecclesiastical leader who has been as close to so many of the people of Canada and the United States as this man.

All people of Polish heritage could share the sentiment of Bishop Zbigniew Kraszenowski of Poland when he said in Rome: "The election of this Pope is like a gold medal put on every Polish Catholic for faithfulness to the church in the past one thousand years." Perhaps this remark is symbolic for Buffalo — in 1969 Mayor Frank A. Sedita presented Cardinal Wojtyla with the keys to the city and a *golden* bison. When the Cardinal returned to Buffalo in 1976 there was a Polish mayor — Stanley M. Makowski.

It was a Buffalo nun, Sister Gracille, who helped Cardinal Wojtyla with his English in preparation for his visits to Canada and the United States, and Sister

Simplicia of Buffalo had the high honour of being chosen to receive Holy Communion from the Pope at the concelebration in Rome.

The photographer Kasprzak had a couple of beers with Cardinal Wojtyla in Buffalo in 1976. It was Polish beer and the Cardinal relished it.

In 1976 the Chopin Singing Society Choir, which has nearly one hundred and fifty members, sang for Cardinal Wojtyla and they have promised to go to Poland to sing for him whenever he travels there.

It seems that nothing can contain the Americans and Dan Kiz of Buffalo, president of the Polish Union of America, told me, "Orchard Lake, Michigan, has a tremendous Polish population who are building a Pope John Paul II Centre at St. Mary's College which will serve as a museum for this historic Pope. It will also be a repository of Polish-American material."

Three Buffalo men were among the thirty-four persons whom President Jimmy Carter sent as delegates to Rome for the investiture of Pope John Paul II. They were Representative John J. LaFalce, Representative Henry J. Nowak and Stan Franczyk.

Cardinal Wojtyla walks through the streets of Buffalo in 1976 with Bishop Head and Monsignor Kazmierczak.

With Bishop Head looking on, Monsignor Kazmierczak kisses the Cardinal's ring.

Others throughout the United States who attended were as follows: Thomas O'Neill, Democrat, Massachusetts, speaker of the House; Zbigniew Brzezinski, national security advisor to the President; Robert F. Wagner, special envoy to the Vatican; Senator Edmund Muskie, Democrat, Maine; Robert Sarros, deputy special envoy to the Vatican; Mrs. Patrick J. Nugent (formerly Luci Baines Johnson); Stanley Milewski, chancellor, Orchard Lake schools, Michigan; Representative Joseph Addabbo, Democrat, New York; Representative Frank Annunzio, Democrat, Illinois; Senator Dewey Bartlett, Republican, Oklahoma; Mathew W. Bieczczat, Cook County commissioner, Illinois; John F. Connally, Crown Cork and Seal Co.; Representative James J. Delaney, Democrat, New York; Representative Edward Derwinski, Republican, Illinois; John Ferro, president, Los Angeles City Council; Governor J. Joseph Garrahy, Rhode Island; Lieutenant Governor Mary Anne Krupsak, New York; Dr. Eugene Kusielewicz, Kosciuszko Foundation; Senator Patrick Leahy, Democrat, Vermont; Raymond Majerus, director, Region 10, United Auto Workers; Aloysius Majewski, president, Polish-American Congress and Polish-American Alliance; Representative Barbara Mikulski, Democrat, Maryland; Azie Taylor Morton, Treasurer of the United States; Representative Lucien Nedzi, Democrat, Michigan; Francis J. O'Connor of O'Connor, Thomas, Hammer, Bentsch & Norby; Representative Dan Rostenkowski, Democrat, Illinois; Jack Spitzer, president, B'Nai Brith International; Dan G. Tapper, former Florida State Senator; John Wojtylo, the Pope's cousin; Representative Clement Zablocki, Democrat, Wisconsin; Representative Leo Zeferetti, Democrat, New York.

The Americans were truly represented.

24

An American's Gift to the Cardinal

Americans love to give lavish presents to important people from abroad. Usually their most extravagant gifts are automobiles, perhaps because people admire American cars or because they are the showpieces of American free enterprise and industry. President Carter gave a sleek auto to Leonid Brezhnev. The American impresario Sol Hurok gave a car to the Soviet dancer Ulanova and Columbia Festivals gave a car to Colonel Podhajsky of the Spanish Riding School of Vienna.

In 1969 an American gave a car to Cardinal Wojtyla.

Edward Arcy was a parishioner of the Divine Child Church in Dearborn, Michigan, a suburb of Detroit. There is also another suburb of Detroit called Orchard Lake where there is a Polish educational and cultural complex. It was there that Arcy met the Cardinal and was impressed by his warm personality and his genuine concern for people. He also heard that because of lack of transportation the Cardinal had difficulty in getting around to see all of his parishioners in Krakow. Arcy talked the matter over with Father Ziemba who was at Orchard Lake in 1969 and who did so much for the visit of the Polish cardinal to the United States.

Arcy made up his mind to give a car to Cardinal Wojtyla.

As reported by Thomas Ewald in the Catholic paper *Our Sunday Visitor*, the Cardinal received a 1970 Ford when he arrived back in Krakow. In later years Arcy even sent parts to maintain the car.

But the Cardinal always saw someone with a need greater than his own. In time he gave the car to a village which he thought needed it more than he did.

Cardinal Wojtyla and Arcy met again in Orchard Lake in 1976.

There were many gifts exchanged among Canadians, Americans and Cardinal Wojtyla, and I have seen some of them in Toronto and Niagara Falls. But there certainly was nothing to match Arcy's gift to the Cardinal who was to become the Polish Pope.

25

The North American Visit of 1976

One of the principal reasons for Cardinal Wojtyla's visit to North America in 1976 was to attend the forty-first International Eucharistic Congress held in Philadelphia from August 1 to 8. The Congress was significant because it was just the second such meeting to be held in the United States. The theme of the Congress evolved from a thought by Archbishop Fulton Sheen, a much revered figure in North America, that today's world is characterized by an erosion of moral standards and a rising demand for social and political justice.

During the time of the congress the Cardinal was a guest in the home of Edward J. Piszek, an outstanding American of Polish heritage. Through this association Ed Piszek persuaded the celebrated American author, James Michener, to go to Krakow to film an interview with Cardinal Wojtyla. By great coincidence the film was aired just after the Cardinal became Pope. So popular was Michener's film, which was really originally Piszek's idea, that viewers asked for it to be repeated again and again.

A kiss from a future Pope. A girl from St. Stanislav Kistka parish in Staten Island, New York, will never forget the kiss she received from Cardinal Wojtyla when she and her classmates greeted him in 1976 at New York's La Guardia Airport.

Scenes from an evening at the St. Stanislaus Parish Credit Union Hall in Toronto. The Cardinal makes a humorous reply to the speeches, chats near the banquet table, takes time for a discussion with author Benedykt Heydenkorn, and renews acquaintance with Zygmunt Jarmicki, organizer of his 1969 trip to Canada.

It was a truly dramatic moment when Ed Piszek first heard that his friend had been elected Pope. He was addressing about sixty people from the government about "Poland's Will to Be" when he was suddenly called to the telephone. He was told that Cardinal Wojtyla had been chosen as Pope. Unbelieving, he said, "Don't say things like that." He thought of Morris West's novel *The Shoes of the*

Fisherman where an Eastern bloc cardinal is elected Pope. Then Piszek rushed back to his audience and announced the news. They gave him a standing ovation.

Ed Piszek and many other people from Philadelphia went to Rome for the investiture of Pope John Paul II.

26

The Pope's Visit to Mexico and the Dominican Republic

People often forget that Mexico is part of North America and should always be considered in discussions about the Western Hemisphere. Furthermore, about sixty million Mexicans, almost double the population of Poland, are Catholics and nearly one-tenth of all Roman Catholics in the world live in Mexico. So it is quite natural that Pope John Paul II would travel to Puebla, Mexico in January of 1979 for the third general assembly of the three hundred Latin American bishops.

A cartoon by Ben Wicks gives some idea of the popularity of Pope John Paul II.

"Unfortunately the Pope has left for Mexico a little earlier than the announced time for our Bon Voyage gathering."

In Mexico City, 1979. Children of Polish descent are lifted to the stand to greet the Pope at the Apostolic Delegation.

On his way to Mexico the Pope stopped at Santo Domingo in the Dominican Republic. This republic lies just off Puerto Rico and shares its island mainland with Haiti.

Just like Columbus, Pope John Paul II arrived in the New World in the West Indies. Did he remember at this time that a Pole, Scolvus, landed in North America long before Columbus did in 1492? Santo Domingo was founded by Bartholomew Columbus, brother of Christopher, and the remains of Christopher Columbus were brought from Spain to rest in its cathedral.

Columbus came to America in the *Santa Maria*; Pope John Paul II came by Concorde jet. No history books record whether Columbus kissed the ground of the New World when he arrived. Pope John Paul made it a day of joy for President Antonio Guzman of the Dominican Republic when he did.

The President said later, "In my opinion Pope John Paul II's visit is perhaps the most important news in the history of the nation."

No foreign visitor to Mexico has received a welcome more tumultuous and warm than that accorded the Pope. Untold millions lined the routes of his processions. Some ten thousand soldiers and policemen acted as security guards when he said Mass at the Shrine of Guadalupe near the capital. In Mexico City a hundred thousand people attended a Mass at Azteca Stadium.

The visit to Puebla projected Pope John Paul II onto the world political scene. His formidable proficiency in the realm of politics was noted by the lay press. *Time* magazine observed that when he "hit the road" he would be performing these skills on a world stage. At the time of the trip to Mexico, Pope John Paul II accepted a request from the presidents of Argentina and Chile to act as mediator in a dispute over the possession of three islands in the Beagle Channel which is at the southern tip of South America.

Pope John Paul II is the second pope to visit Latin America. Pope Paul VI travelled to Colombia in 1968, just one year before Cardinal Wojtyla visited Canada and the United States. Since then an angry debate has arisen in the church over priestly activism in Latin America. Although the majority of bishops are conservative, some of the younger priests and missionaries responded to governmental oppression of their people by embracing Marxist economic ideas under the banner of "liberation theology." Vatican experts estimate that since 1968 at least one thousand priests and bishops have suffered interrogation, imprisonment, torture or murder. Pope John Paul II endorsed the "theology of liberation" and stressed that it should be taken up by the church throughout the

A group of mounted "charros," Mexican cowboys, escort Pope John Paul II in his open motorcade through the streets of Mexico City in January, 1979. The charros were armed with the traditional sabre-like machetes and inlaid .39 pistols.

world, but he also warned against partisan political activism by priests and against advocating Marxist themes of class struggle, violence and hatred of the rich in the struggle of the poor to end oppression.

Poland and Mexico share many similar features. Nearly all the people in both countries are Roman Catholic and they hold a special veneration for the Virgin Mary, yet there is complete separation between the state and the church. In Poland this receives a great deal of publicity because the government is Communist whereas it is not in Mexico. In fact, the Communist party has only recently been made legal in Mexico. Religious education is prohibited in the schools of both countries.

Clerics are much more severely dealt with in Mexico than in Poland. As an example, a priest is not permitted to wear religious garb outside of church. When the Pope arrived in Mexico, however, the church bells tolled in defiance of the law and the Mexican bishops paraded openly in their ecclesiastical clothing.

When the Pope arrived in Mexico he kissed the ground at the airport, an airport named for a Mexican, Benito Juarez, who had been excommunicated from the church. Someone presented him with a sombrero and he put it on briefly, which possibly no other pope in history would have done. It was like a symbolic gesture to show that it was time to discard some old ways in Mexico.

How could the Mexicans not take this man to their hearts, particularly when it is remembered that in preparation for this trip the Pope arose at five every morning to brush up on his Spanish?

What would be the result if political leaders and others took the time and made the effort to speak to people around the world in their own tongue? Certainly Americans could learn a little Spanish to deal with their millions of Mexican immigrants and we in Canada could learn a little French to communicate with our French-speaking citizens.

His Holiness perhaps speeded his journey from Santo Domingo to Mexico City when he heard that a "passionate cooking Pole" was preparing a real Polish meal for him.

This meal, prepared by Tadeusz Podbereski, was to consist of "Bigos," a hunter's stew of sweet and sour cabbage with eight kinds of fresh and smoked meats and sausages, which Poles have eaten for eight hundred years. I have sampled this stew at the Sir Nicholas restaurant in Toronto and the Bristol Hotel in Warsaw. For the dish to reach perfection three days are required for its preparation.

That was the main course but the Pope's appetizer was another traditional offering, nozki w galaretce, or pig's feet in jelly.

Of course the soup had to be barszcz, one of the best soups in the world. It is a beet soup with many other vegetables. It sometimes includes mushrooms, usually Polish mushrooms, which are the most delicious to be found anywhere. Poles and Jews make the barszcz clear but Ukrainians and Russians make it with sour cream.

Dessert was szarkitjay, a Polish apple pie, and faworki, something like a cruller which is pre-Lenten fare.

In Canada and the United States the Pope drank beer but Podbereski offered him Zubrowka, a Polish vodka flavoured with aromatic grasses from the plains in Poland where the wild buffalo herd.

A meal like that is enough to bring anyone to Mexico!

Latin America holds almost one half of all the world's Catholics. Through his visit Pope John Paul II was acknowledging this fact.

The Pope and his Church have survived the Nazi occupation and the Communist takeover of his own country. Surely they will survive both oppression and rebelliousness in Latin America.

27

Poland in June 1979

In June 1979 thousands of Canadians and Americans will flock to Poland when Pope John Paul II will again visit his native country. His visit was originally scheduled for May 1979, the celebration of the nine hundredth anniversary of the death of St. Stanislaus, the patron saint of the country. St. Stanislaus (my name saint) was the first son of Poland to be canonized. He was slain in 1079 by the order of King Boleslaus because he upheld his Catholic faith. He was murdered in the cathedral in Krakow where Pope John Paul II was later to be archbishop and cardinal for seventeen years.

The Communist authorities feared that there would be a mass patriotic uprising by the people of Poland if Pope John Paul II were to be in Poland at the time of the celebrations so his visit was put off until June.

In 1969 Cardinal Wojtyla, now Pope John Paul II, gave the following address to Canadians and Americans of Polish descent.

"Who are you?

"You are children of Poles who left their homeland for various reasons to come to Canada and the United States to find a new place.

"You were born into this new world but from early childhood you learned your parents' language as well as the language of Canadians and Americans. Maybe for you it is easiest to express yourself in the language of your new countries when your parents' language becomes difficult. Nevertheless your heredity is there in your parents' homeland, left behind so many years ago.

"You discover in yourself a feeling of attachment to this original homeland, you discover Polishness which is the deepest foundation of your soul. We have heard that after visiting Poland you return to America deeply moved and with stronger feelings for this attachment . . . one such girl said, 'Now I know what it means to have two homelands.'

"So your identity is that you are Poles, but if Canadians, then Canadians of Polish descent; if Americans, Americans of Polish descent.

"We wish you to retain your identity, discovering and expressing your Polishness — particularly your heritage from your parents — and we wish you to be aware of the binding consequences and conclusions arising from this heritage.

"Perhaps these consequences and conclusions will be stronger with you than with older generations."

Oh, to be in Krakow!

Oh, to be with Him!

Picture Credits

We would like to express our thanks to those who gave us permission to reproduce photographs and drawings, as follows:

Art Photo Studio, Toronto — 60, 61. Colour – II, bottom left and
   right; III (4 photos); IV – bottom; V – top left and bottom.

Adam Bujak, Artysta Fotografik, Krakow — 32 (2 photos), 33

Canadian Press — 12

Father Joseph Capiga, Hamilton, Ontario — 68, 69, 70

Andy Donato, *Toronto Sun* — 20

W. B. Edwards, Inc., St. Jean, Québec — 49 (right)

Foto Felici, Roma — Colour – VII, bottom left; VIII, bottom

The Hamilton Spectator — 66

Hayward Studios, Inc., Montreal — 53

Edward L. Kasprzak, Buffalo, N.Y. — 77, 78, 79, 80. Colour – I;
   VIII, top

Janusz Kolasa, Lublin — 2 (4 photos), 7, 8, 9 (3 photos),
   10 (3 photos), 34, 35, 43, 44

Stan Kowalski, Ottawa — 56 (2 photos)

Le Soleil, Québec — 50 (left)

W. H. Leppek, Toronto — 28 (4 photos), 30, 40, 62, 63, 83 (4 photos);
   Colour – VI (3 photos)

Arturo Mari, *L'Osservatore Romano*, Citta del Vaticano — 36

La Ville de Montréal — 49 (left), 52 (2 photos)

NC Photo (from Canadian Press) — 23, 82, 86

Stan Obodiac — 46

Oshawa Times — 64

Ponitificia Fotografia Felici, Roma — 24

La Ville de Québec — 50 (right)

Geoffrey Saville-Read — 51; Colour – IV (top)

Bill Simpkins, *Calgary Herald* — 58

Ted Stelmaszynski, Niagara Falls, Ontario — 73, 74; Colour – V (top right)

Ben Wicks, *The Globe and Mail* — 85